SURREY
PUB WALKS

Matthew Ogborn

COUNTRYSIDE BOOKS
NEWBURY BERKSHIRE

Shere

First published 2023
© 2023 Matthew Ogborn

All rights reserved. No part of this publication may be reproduced, stored in a retrieval system, or transmitted by any means, electronic, mechanical, photocopying, recording or otherwise, without the prior written permission of the copyright holder and publishers.

COUNTRYSIDE BOOKS
3 Catherine Road
Newbury, Berkshire

To view our complete range of books,
please visit us at
www.countrysidebooks.co.uk

ISBN 978 1 84674 412 9

All materials used in the manufacture of this book carry FSC certification

Title page illustration by Andy Fairburn

Produced through The Letterworks Ltd., Reading
Designed and Typeset by KT Designs, St Helens
Printed by The Holywell Press, Oxford

Contents

Area map   5
Introduction   6

WALK

1 Farnham – The Botanist, The Nelson Arms   8
   and The Hop Blossom (*2½ miles*)
2 Frensham – The Holly Bush (*5 miles*)   12
3 Virginia Water – The Belvedere Arms (*4 miles*)   17
4 West End – The Inn at West End (*2¼ miles*)   21
5 Pirbright – The Royal Oak (*2 or 4 miles*)   25

6	West Clandon – The Onslow Arms (4¾ *miles*)	29
7	Guildford – The Drummond, The Royal Oak and The Weyside (3½ *miles*)	34
8	Shere – The William Bray (3½ *miles*)	39
9	Wonersh – The Grantley Arms (3 *miles*)	43
10	Godalming & Farncombe – The Cricketers and The Star (3 *miles*)	48
11	Chiddingfold – The Crown Inn (3 *miles*)	53
12	Surbiton & Kingston – The Spring Grove, The Albion and The Antelope (3 *miles*)	58
13	Epsom Common – The Jolly Coopers (2¼ *miles*)	63
14	Headley – The Cock Inn (4 *miles*)	67
15	Leigh – The Plough (2¾ *miles*)	71
16	Coldharbour – The Plough Inn (3½ *miles*)	75
17	Forest Green – The Parrot (3 *miles*)	80
18	Coulsdon – The Rambler's Rest (2¼ *miles*)	84
19	Bletchingley – The Bletchingley Arms (4 *miles*)	88
20	Limpsfield Chart – The Carpenters Arms (3 *miles*)	92

Virginia Water

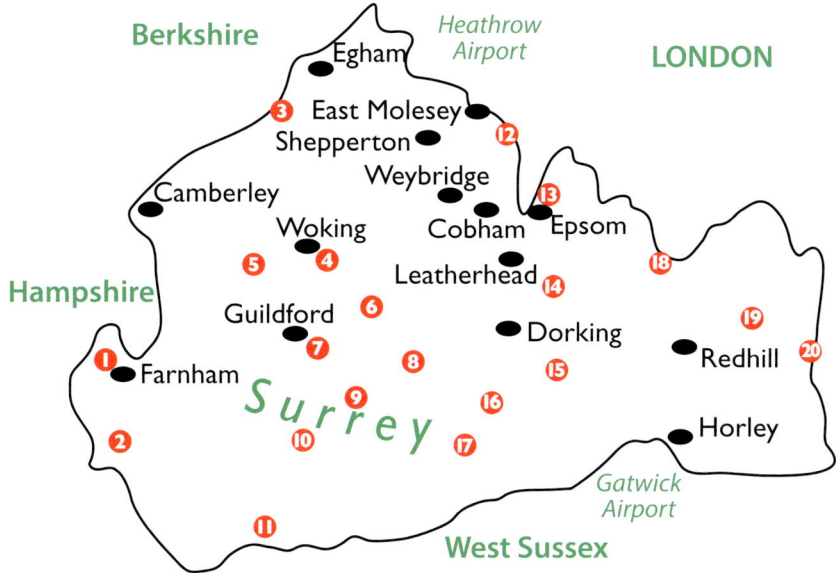

PUBLISHER'S NOTE

We hope that you obtain considerable enjoyment from this book; great care has been taken in its preparation. Although at the time of publication all routes followed public rights of way or permitted paths, diversion orders can be made and permissions withdrawn.

We cannot, of course, be held responsible for such diversion orders or any inaccuracies in the text which result from these or any other changes to the routes, nor any damage which might result from walkers trespassing on private property. We are anxious, though, that all the details covering the walks are kept up to date, and would therefore welcome information from readers which would be relevant to future editions.

The simple sketch maps that accompany the walks in this book are based on notes made by the author whilst surveying the routes on the ground. However, for the benefit of a proper map, we do recommend that you purchase the relevant Ordnance Survey sheet covering your walk.

INTRODUCTION

I always thought I knew Surrey pretty well. My mother grew up in Stoneleigh, my Dad moved down from east London, my brother and I were born in Epsom, and my wife moved here so we could start a family in Surbiton.

Then I started researching this book and realised I was wrong. I quickly discovered I'd only scratched the surface. In the process of mapping these walks, my travels to all four corners of the county highlighted how wonderfully diverse Surrey is in terms of geography, geology, flora, fauna and, of course, pubs.

Whether it's the stunning mixture of landscapes on the Frensham walk, the long history of The Crown Inn in Chiddingfold or the vibrant community hub that is The Plough Inn in Coldharbour, surrounded by some of the most amazing views in England, if you take the time to explore the county properly, you will be richly rewarded.

In compiling this book, I felt spoilt for choice. The only difficulty lay in deciding which walks to include. Some (captivating routes around places like Oxshott Common or Friday Street) were hamstrung by the lack of a nearby pub; in other cases, I found brilliant pubs that didn't have walks long or varied enough to warrant inclusion. The walks that did make it truly deserve their place here.

The majority of these walks can be reached by both private and public transport, making them accessible to all. I have also taken care to not just cater to ramblers, but dog walkers, families, young hikers and children.

The walks vary in distance and topography with some being a quick cobweb-cleaner, and others a more challenging workout that will leave you satisfied and invigorated by the time you settle down for a hearty meal at the pub.

Speaking of pubs, there are plenty of diverse options here – from award-winning newcomers to old favourites that have been serving their local community for generations. Hopefully these outings will tempt people from further afield; after all, most of the locations are less than an hour down from London or up from the coast by car, train or bus, and there's the opportunity to sample produce from local craft beer breweries, gin distilleries and vineyards, as well as sumptuous food using local ingredients.

For safety reasons, I recommend that you undertake the more challenging walks in the company of other people, while it is always wise to be prepared by looking at the weather forecast beforehand to ensure that you have adequate clothing along with a bottle of water and a first aid kit. Please be considerate of other walkers, joggers, bikers and horse riders, especially if you are wearing earphones, as some of the walks are more isolated than others. Naturally, some of the walks will pose a stiffer test in the winter months or following spells of heavy rain.

More than anything, I hope you get as much enjoyment out of the winding walks and inviting pubs as I did while putting this book together.

Matthew Ogborn

ACKNOWLEDGEMENTS

For my Surrey family, whose support, love and understanding fuelled this book, the people who joined me for laughter on the walks and my publishers Alex Batho and Rory Batho for showing faith and immense patience. It took a while, but we got it done eventually!

Big thanks to the people who did the walks with me… Kate Thomis Ogborn, Theo Ogborn, Edie Ogborn, Terence Ogborn, Stephen Kinsella, Daniel McCrohan, Miles Evans, Jon Francis, Daniel Morgan, Faye Morgan, Mabel Morgan, Noah Morgan and Martin Jackson.

Books used for reference
The Story of Forest Green by Kathleen M. Baker
Surrey A County History by John Janaway
Ordnance Survey Historical Guides: Surrey by Dennis Turner
Hidden Surrey: Town & Country by Chris Howkins
Guildford: A History & Celebration by Russell Chamberlin
The Kingston Book by June Sampson

Walk 1
Farnham

Distance: 2½ miles (4 km)

Start: Farnham Railway Station, Farnham, GU9 8AG.

How to get there: Farnham is easy to travel to by road via the A31 or roads such as Folly Hill to the north, Waverley Lane to the east, Frensham Road to the south and Crondall Lane to the west. There is a good South Western Railway service operating from London Waterloo all the way to Alton in the south, while several regular buses are also available.

Parking: Farnham Station multi-storey car park.

Map: OS Explorer 145: Guildford & Farnham.
Grid Ref: SU843465.

This Farnham walk is the most westerly in the book and a short, fun one. It's also an opportunity to explore a charming town full of history, while the three pubs featured should provide enough variety to please even the most picky of drinkers and foodies.

Farnham ①

THE PUB — **THE BOTANIST** is the first stop on the leisurely route with the chain venue something a little different from others in this book. One of 25 around the country, it is situated next to the excellent Blue Bear Bookshop on The Borough. They offer a tasty spread of starters, mains and their trademark hanging kebabs, while resident botanists craft unusual concoctions behind the bar. ⊕ www.thebotanist.uk.com ☎ 01252 718089.

THE PUB — **THE NELSON ARMS** on Castle Street is the middle stop on this walk. This atmospheric, timber-beamed pub was originally three farm cottages on the Farnham Castle estate. The present name is based on Admiral Horatio Nelson's reported visits to the town to see his paramour, Lady Hamilton, who lived on nearby Firgrove Hill. The menu is packed full of pub favourites with a comprehensive wine choice and beers on tap. ⊕ www.thenelsonarmsfarnham.co.uk ☎ 01252 727222.

THE PUB — **THE HOP BLOSSOM** on Long Garden Walk is the third pub. The open fire is a big draw in winter, while the sunny outside tables are perfect for warmer months. Real ale fans flock to it due to its Master Cellarman status. ⊕ www.hopblossom.co.uk ☎ 01252 710770.

The Walk

❶ Head out of the train station, and left down **Station Hill** crossing at the traffic lights of the **A31/Farnham bypass** into **South Street**. The first point of interest is **The Haren Garden**, marked by a plaque, on the right-hand side of the road after you cross over the **River Wey**. Keep on going up **South Street**, past **Farnham Methodist Church**, until you meet the junction of the **A325** and **The Borough**. Turn left and cross over to walk on the right-hand side of the street, passing **The Botanist** as you go. At **Castle Street** turn right up the historic street until you reach **Long Garden Walk** on the left. If you wish to visit the **Nelson Arms** keep ahead on **Castle Street**; the pub is just past **Park Row** on the right. Then retrace your steps to **Long Garden Walk**.

❷ To continue the walk, head down the alleyway, which opens up more the nearer you get to **The Hop Blossom**. As **Long**

Surrey Pub Walks

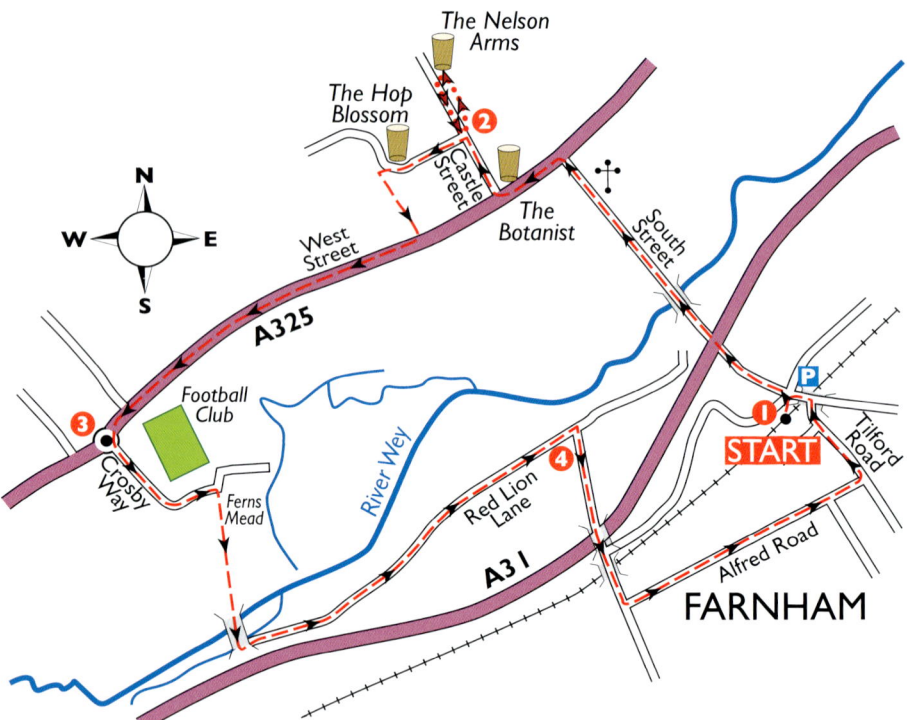

Garden Walk bears right, turn left into **Lion and Lamb Way** and immediately left down **Lion and Lamb Yard**. When you reach the bottom of the cobbles, turn right into the **West Street** part of the A325 and follow this all the way down to the roundabout.

❸ Turn left down **Crosby Way** past **Farnham Town Football Club**, until you reach a junction. Turn right down **Whitlet Close** and continue on the footpath that cuts across **Ferns Mead**, a welcome dose of greenery in the urban stroll. Cross over the bridge that spans two branches of the **River Wey**, then turn left down **Weydon Mill Lane**, which becomes **Red Lion Lane**. Keep going past the church until you reach **Farnham Maltings** and a road junction.

❹ Turn hard right up **Firgrove Hill**. This takes you back over the A31/Farnham bypass to **Alfred Road** on the left-hand side.

Farnham

Follow **Alfred Road** past its large houses until the end of the road. Turn left into **Tilford Road**, which takes you back to the station car park, train or other transport.

Places of Interest Nearby

Farnham is one of the five largest conurbations in Surrey with the historic market town first granted a market and fair in 1216. The monthly farmers' market is still very popular, while the **Farnham Maltings arts centre** hosts a monthly market selling arts, crafts, antiques and bric-a-brac. ⊕ farnhammaltings.com

Farnham Castle Keep, which sits on the crest of a hill overlooking the town, is free to enter. Most of the Surrey fighting during the English Civil War centred around the Bishop of Winchester's Farnham Castle, which was of immense strategic value to both sides as it guarded important roads up from the west to London.
⊕ english-heritage.org.uk/visit/places/farnham-castle-keep

Walk 2
FRENSHAM

Distance: 5 miles (8 km)

Start: The Holly Bush, Shortfield Common Road, Frensham, GU10 3BJ.

How to get there: The Holly Bush is 10 minutes' drive south of the A31 with easy access from the north and south via the A287, Shortfield Common Road to the west and the Reeds Road from the east. Alternatively you can get a taxi from Farnham train station to the north that takes about eight minutes, while the 19 bus operates between Aldershot and Haslemere.

Parking: Park at the pub if visiting, or roadside on Shortfield Common Road.

Map: OS Explorer 145: Guildford & Farnham.
Grid Ref: SU843422.

A beautiful route that takes in several different landscapes in all their glory. This is the longest walk in the book, but the elevation

Frensham 2

shouldn't present too much of a challenge. Cutting through the magnificent Frensham Common, which could double for the southern French coast in parts thanks to its sandy nature, it skirts both Frensham Little Pond and Frensham Great Pond as well as the lovely Frensham village itself.

THE PUB **THE HOLLY BUSH** is an intriguing mix of rustic furniture and contemporary lighting inside, with large benches sheltered under a wooden canopy outside. Their brunch menu is very popular, while their lunch and dinner menu is a gamut of tasty small dishes and sandwiches, along with burgers, fish, meat and veggie options plus fun kids' options. Wines are from independent vineyards with two local ales on tap at the bar and coffee beans supplied by Horsham Coffee Roasters.
⊕ www.thehollybush.co.uk ☎ 01252 447060.

The Walk

❶ From **The Holly Bush** head right, down **Shortfield Common Road**. When you reach the end of the houses on the left, turn left down the footpath that travels along the back of them. When the **Hollowdene Recreation Ground** appears on your left, bear right following the footpath nearest to the **River Wey** on your right. When you get down to the bottom, turn left with the woods on your right then turn right and follow the footpath towards the **A287**. Turn right along the pavement, over the bridge that crosses the River Wey and cross over into **Priory Lane**. Follow the lane round to the right, then when it turns back left, leave the lane and keep ahead to a footpath.

❷ Take the first left onto a footpath that runs parallel with the lane and takes you into the spellbinding **Frensham Common**. Head to the end of the car park on your left, then turn right past **Pond Cottage** to **Frensham Little Pond** where you can take a moment to watch the swans and other birds. After that, follow the footpath with Little Pond on your left and the beach area where people flock in summer to soak up the holiday feel. When you get to a junction of six paths at the end of Little Pond, head straight over and up, then take a left at the second path junction. Follow the path until you reach the trees, then turn left along

Surrey Pub Walks

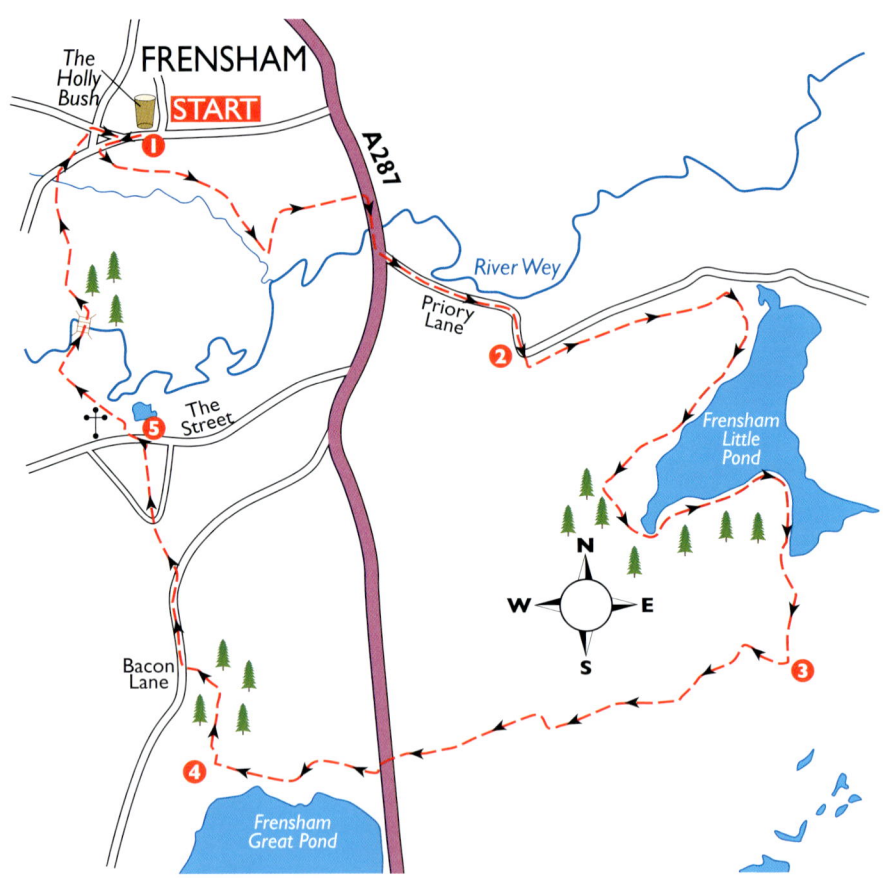

the footpath that follows the southern edge of Little Pond before you emerge back onto the Common again. Follow the footpath round to the right, keeping the trees on your left.

❸ The next section can be tricky with a number of footpath options. You need to head in the general direction of **Frensham Great Pond**. Turn right at the next junction and left at the next. Cross over the main footpath with the trees on your left, pass by the first footpath on your right by **Smugglers** and take the second footpath on your right. Keep going to the next junction where you take a right and then left onto another heather-lined footpath that provides an amazing view down towards the Great

Frensham 2

Pond. Breathe in the country air and amble down to the A287 where you need to take care when crossing. Once on the other side, follow the footpath initially, then turn left down nearer the Great Pond which has a larger beach area for families to enjoy in the sunnier months.

4 Turn right behind **Frensham Pond Snack Bar** and take the footpath through the woods up until the next junction, when you turn left and cut across the bridleway up to **Bacon Lane**. Listen out for traffic on this next stretch as you will need to turn right on the road for about 200 metres until you reach a footpath on your left. Cut down that and follow it through the middle of the houses in Frensham village up to **The Street**.

5 Cross the road and take the track on the right of the **St Mary the Virgin church** – home to a large cauldron said to have been borrowed from the fairies and never returned – all the way down to the end. Turn right onto the footpath at the end which borders the River Wey again and looks up at the houses above in **Spreakley**. Cross over the small bridge and take the footpath on

Surrey Pub Walks

the left, that has the woods on your right, up and over another track. Continue along the footpath behind the back of **Spreakley House** up to **Shortfield Common Road**. Cross over onto the village green and bear right up to **Broomfield Lane** where you turn right to return to the **Holly Bush**.

Places of Interest Nearby

Frensham is known primarily for **Frensham Common**, owned by the National Trust and a Site of Special Scientific Interest (SSSI). It lies on the bank of the **River Wey**, with **Frensham Great Pond** and **Frensham Little Pond** built in the Middle Ages to provide fish for the Bishop of Winchester's estate. Having been drained in the Second World War, they were later transformed into a leisure destination.

Walk 3
Virginia Water

Distance: 4 miles (6.6 km)

Start: The Belvedere Arms, London Road, Sunninghill, SL5 7SB.

How to get there: Even though the pub is in Berkshire, the walk cuts across the county border to Surrey and is easily accessible on London Road, 10 minutes west from Junction 12 of the M25 and Junction 2 of the M3. The nearest railway stations are a five-minute taxi ride away with Ascot to the west, Sunningdale to the south and Virginia Water to the east between London Waterloo and Reading on South Western Railway, and with the No. 1 bus nearby.

Parking: Park at the pub if visiting, or Blacknest Car Park which is a little further along London Road.

Map: OS Explorer 160: Windsor, Weybridge & Bracknell.
Grid Ref: SU958687.

Surrey Pub Walks

This is a truly beautiful walk, especially when everything is in bloom in the sunnier months. The most north-westerly walk in this book, it straddles the county line between Surrey and Berkshire. With a gentle first half that then rises a little up into the Valley Gardens and down again, it's a magical mix of greenery and water, and perfect for all ages.

THE PUB — **THE BELVEDERE ARMS** is well reviewed with seasonal menus and an eclectic range of wines, real ales and lagers on offer into the bargain. The good-sized menu includes a weekend brunch selection along with sandwiches and British favourites. Recently refurbished with stylish interiors, it boasts an attractive outdoor space perfect for a drink or al fresco dining in the sunshine. ⊕ www.belvederearms.co.uk ☎ 01344 870931.

The Walk

1 With your back to the pub turn right and then right again up **Blacknest Gate Road** to **Blacknest Gate**. Veer right following the path down over the bridge and then turn left onto the footpath with the water to your left and **Frostfarm Plantation** to your right. Meander along this idyllic stretch until you reach the **First Pond Head** photo spot with **Leptis Magna Roman Ruins** stretching back up to your right. Once you've had a look,

Virginia Water 3

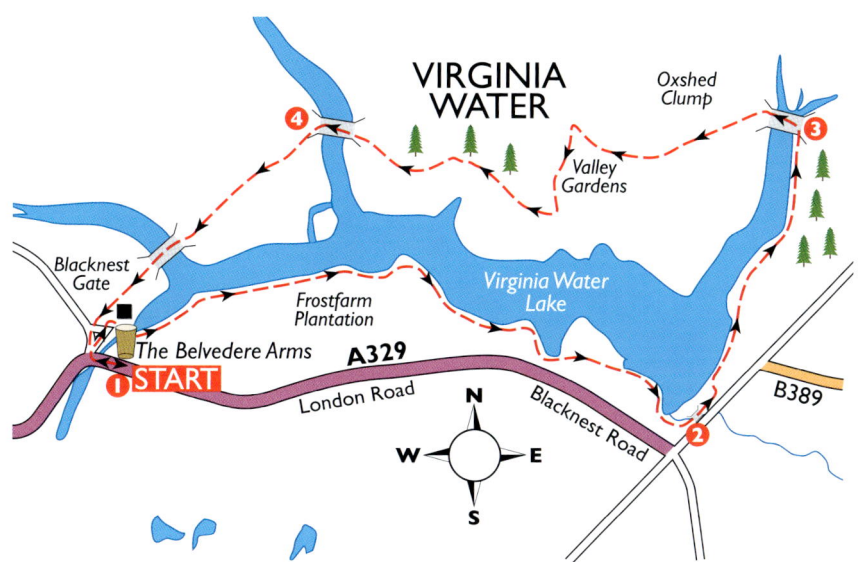

continue on to the **Cascade waterfall** up near **London Road** which is a perfect place to stop and take a few photos.

2 Next, go over the **Cascade Bridge** and stay alongside the water as the footpath bends north towards **Virginia Water Lake Pavilion** where you can grab a drink or take a toilet stop. Carry on along the footpath up past the **Virginia Water Plantations** and **Enchanted Forest** to your right until you get to the bridge with **Wick Pond** to your right.

3 Head left over the bridge to arrive at the **Totem Pole**, another good photo opportunity. When you're ready take the path that points up towards the **Valley Gardens**. This goes up and bends right past **Oxshed Clump** on your right until you reach a junction where you need to turn hard left so you travel back down through a stunning parade of bushes, flowers and trees with the **Punch Bowl** up above to your left. Head down until you reach the first large track, then turn right and follow that until you get past the trees and over a clearing, where you meet a footpath.

Surrey Pub Walks

4 Turn left here and continue over the bridge, then bear left over the grassy footpath that takes you down to **High Bridge**. Cross over there, then follow the last stretch of track along **Queen Victoria's Avenue** down to **Blacknest Gate**. Retrace your steps back down **Blacknest Gate Road** to return to the pub or **Blacknest car park**.

Places of Interest Nearby

Virginia Water was a stream that grew in the 18th century into the large lake of today, with the River Bourne feeding it and exiting at the eastern end after the ornamental **Cascade waterfall**. Its perimeter is about 4½ miles (7.2 km) with half paved and the other half natural. It might look familiar, having been used as a filming location for the Harry Potter films and *Into the Woods*.

Walk 4
WEST END

Distance: 2¼ miles (3.6 km)

Start: The Inn at West End, 42 Guildford Road, West End, GU24 9PW.

How to get there: The Inn at West End is located on the A322 six minutes southeast from Junction 3 of the M3 with access south down to Bisley and beyond, west via the B311 and east on the A319. It is eight minutes by taxi from Bagshot railway station to the north and Brookwood railway to the south, while you can get there using both the 34 and 35 buses.

Parking: Park at the pub if visiting, or roadside on the High Street opposite. Note this is one way so you'll need to follow the main road round to the right and right again to reach it.

Map: OS Explorer 145: Guildford & Farnham.
Grid Ref: SU945610.

Surrey Pub Walks

This gentle 45-minute stroll through charming woods and heathland makes for an excellent family walk suitable for all ages. There are cracking views back across the military areas of West End Common and Pirbright Common, while The Inn at West End boasts a beautiful vine-covered courtyard and boutique accommodation if required.

THE INN AT WEST END is part of the enterprising Barons Pub Company chain. The dog-friendly pub serves award-winning food with an excellent breakfast menu, while lunch includes British favourites as well as a vegetarian and vegan selection. Their Sunday roasts draw a large crowd, so be sure to book. ⊕ www.baronspubs.com/innatwestend
☎ 01276 858652.

West End 4

The Walk

1 Head left from the pub and left again down **Brentmoor Road** for a few metres. Cross over onto the footpath left of the woods then, after you pass over a track, bear right down the twisty footpath that takes you through into the woods with houses on the left and **Sandpit Hill** to your right. Cross over a bridleway and up another footpath through woods until you see some New England-style houses.

2 Follow the path behind the houses and over a bridleway onto another bridleway that passes through the woods on the ridge line. When you get to the end of the bridleway and the start of the **Greyspot Hill military area**, take a moment to soak in the hypnotic views back down over the wide expanse of heathland.

3 Turn left down the scenic bridleway that borders the military area to a small, wooded bridge that marks the edge of **Brentmoor Heath**. Turn left here over the bridge and wind your way through an open expanse of land that can sometimes get a little boggy with persistent rain. Keep to the right-hand

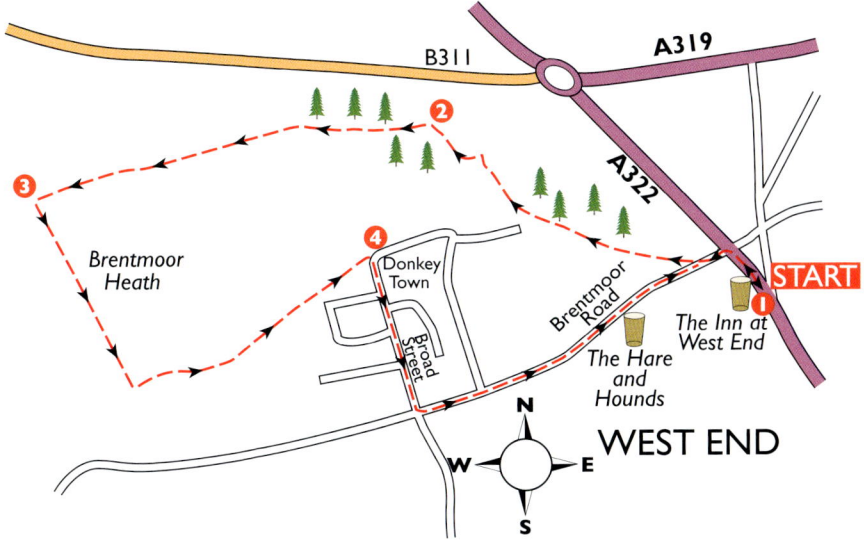

23

Surrey Pub Walks

footpath through Brentmoor Heath towards the **Donkey Town residential estate**. Take the footpath behind it up to the corner of **Birch Lane**.

❹ Turn right down **Broad Street** past the houses until you get to the junction with **Brentmoor Road**. Turn left and follow the road for ½ mile, past the **Hare and Hounds**, until you reach **Guildford Road**, where you turn right to return to the pub.

Places of Interest Nearby

West End is midway between the towns of **Camberley** and **Woking**, while the **River Bourne** rises from its sources to the west through the village. The village is known mostly for **West End Common**, which includes **British Army training ranges** and is home to rare heathland plants making it a designated **Site of Special Scientific Interest** (SSSI).

Walk 5
PIRBRIGHT

Distance: 2 or 4 miles (3.4 or 6.5 km)

Start: The Royal Oak, Aldershot Road, Pirbright, GU24 0DQ.

How to get there: The Royal Oak is located about 10 minutes from the A331 to the west on the A324/Pirbright Road that runs up from through to Pirbright itself, while the B380 heads out east towards Mayford. The nearest railway station is about six minutes by taxi from Brookwood to the north and around eight minutes from Worplesdon to the east, coming from London Waterloo on South Western Railway down to Alton for the former, and Portsmouth for the latter. The 28 bus runs past regularly with the 48 bus route also nearby to the north.

Parking: Park at the pub with permission from the landlord.

Map: OS Explorer 145: Guildford & Farnham.
Grid Ref: SU944543.

This is a gem of a walk in an underrated part of the county. The route clocks in at just over four miles and will get your lungs working on a first-half ascent that takes you up to Crown Prince

Surrey Pub Walks

Hill on the edge of a military area. The scenic walk back down through some striking wooded areas is a welcome respite before you head to The Royal Oak for refreshments.

Note: The longer route crosses a military training shooting range and should not be attempted during firing times or when the red flags and/or lights are hoisted. Please follow the shorter route if this is the case. An internet search for 'Ash Ranges Firing Times' will give you closing times.

THE PUB **THE ROYAL OAK** is a popular local pub, and part of the Greene King chain. The weekend brunches and large Sunday roast selection are a big hit, so it's worth booking ahead. Behind the bar you'll find local ales from the likes of Hogs Back Brewery. The huge beer garden is a boon in the sunnier months, with live acoustic music played on Saturdays during the summer. ⊕ www.greeneking-pubs.co.uk/pubs/surrey/royal-oak-pirbright ☎ 01483 232466.

The Walk

1 Head left out of **The Royal Oak** and across **Aldershot Road** to the track on the right-hand side of the road that leads into the woods with **Stream Farm** to your right. Follow this

Pirbright 5

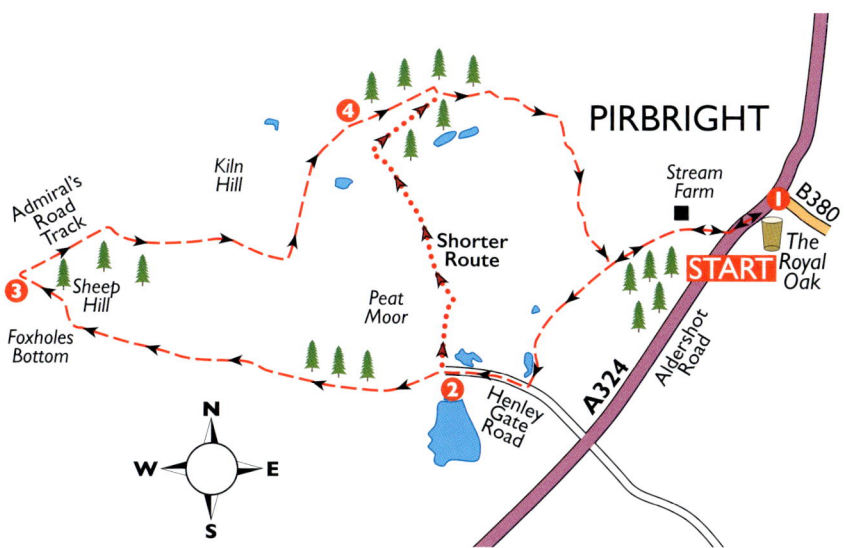

path for just over ½ mile, past **Bourne House** and **West Stream House** on your right, to **Henley Gate road**. Turn right and walk up to the gate that enters the military shooting range and danger area that makes up the middle section of the walk. If the red flags and/or lights are hoisted do not enter the training area. Instead, turn right and follow the path through the kissing gate and straight ahead. Cross a stile and go through a gate, keeping ahead on the clear path. In around ½ mile the path reaches a junction. Go through the gate and turn right (**Mill Lane**). Follow this lane until you reach the back of **The Duchies Cottage** where you can pick up the walk from point 4.

❷ If the danger area is not in use and therefore safe to enter, keep the military shooting range on your left, head along the track opposite signed permissive path keeping the fence directly to your left, passing briefly through a wooded area until you come out into the open heathland. Gird your lungs for a slow and steady ascent up the sandy track to **Long Hill** stopping to admire the colourful flora and fauna that spreads out all around you. Keep going on the track that cuts between **Foxholes Bottom** and **Sheep Hill** until you reach the bottom of **Crown Prince Hill** where you can admire the breathtaking views.

Surrey Pub Walks

3 Turn right down **Admiral's Road** track with the trees on your right, and then take the first track on your right. Walk down with the trees on your left until you reach the big fence that encircles the military area. Turn left with **Kiln Hill** up to your left and follow the fence around to the right until you reach a big swing gate at the end of the Admiral's Road track.

4 Go through the gate, then head left until you come to a junction which you cross to reach the back of a field to your right. Follow the path behind **The Duchies Cottage**. At the junction follow the footpath opposite, then turn right through the rhododendron woods down another footpath. Carry on under the trees, then over two streams that can become very boggy after persistent rain and back to the track you followed earlier in the walk. Turn left back to **Aldershot Road** and over to the pub.

Places of Interest Nearby

Pirbright has an interesting backstory with the area being part of the **Royal Hunting Forest of Windsor** and the **manor** part of the dowry of Queen Katharine of Aragon during the reign of Henry VIII. The **Basingstoke Canal** opened in 1794 to divide the parish into two areas, while the Army purchased large areas in the 1870s leading to the extensive Ministry of Defence land seen today which is used by the **Army Training Centre Pirbright**.

Colin Smith

Walk 6
WEST CLANDON

Distance: 4¾ miles (7.6 km)

Start: The Onslow Arms, The Street, West Clandon, GU4 7TE.

How to get there: The Onslow Arms is located in West Clandon on the A247 and is easily accessed from the A3 to the north and the A25 to the south with parking available at the back. Clandon railway station is right by the pub with trains shuttling between London Waterloo, Epsom and Guildford, while there are buses which you can take from places like Woking and Guildford.

Parking: Park at the pub if visiting, or at Clandon Station a little further along The Street.

Map: OS Explorer 145: Guildford & Farnham.
Grid Ref: TQ045523.

Surrey Pub Walks

This is one of the longest walks in the book at nearly five miles with a total ascent of 379ft. However, it's fairly gradual and family-friendly if you have time on your hands. The pasture, views back towards the famous Clandon House and stunning tree-lined path after Wildwood make for an interesting visual mix.

THE PUB — **THE ONSLOW ARMS** is a popular destination for foodies, with a separate dining room, comfortable bar areas and attractive patio that draws in punters from far and wide. Their menu includes the pick of British classics made with seasonal ingredients, as well as hearty Sunday roasts and vegan-friendly dishes. Bonus points for the wines sourced from local vineyards.
🌐 www.onslowarmsclandon.co.uk ☎ 01483 222447.

The Walk

❶ Head left out of the **Onslow Arms** and down **The Street**, taking care on the narrow pavements. If you have parked at the station, you will also turn left onto **The Street**, passing the pub as you go. Keep going for around ½ mile, passing a primary school and the **Bulls Head pub**, then turn right down a wide downhill path.

❷ Keep the field to your right, then turn left through the wood and amble over a bridge that crosses the lake at the back of **Clandon Park house**. Proceed over a field and across the path up to the right of the farm. Keep ahead. There may

West Clandon 6

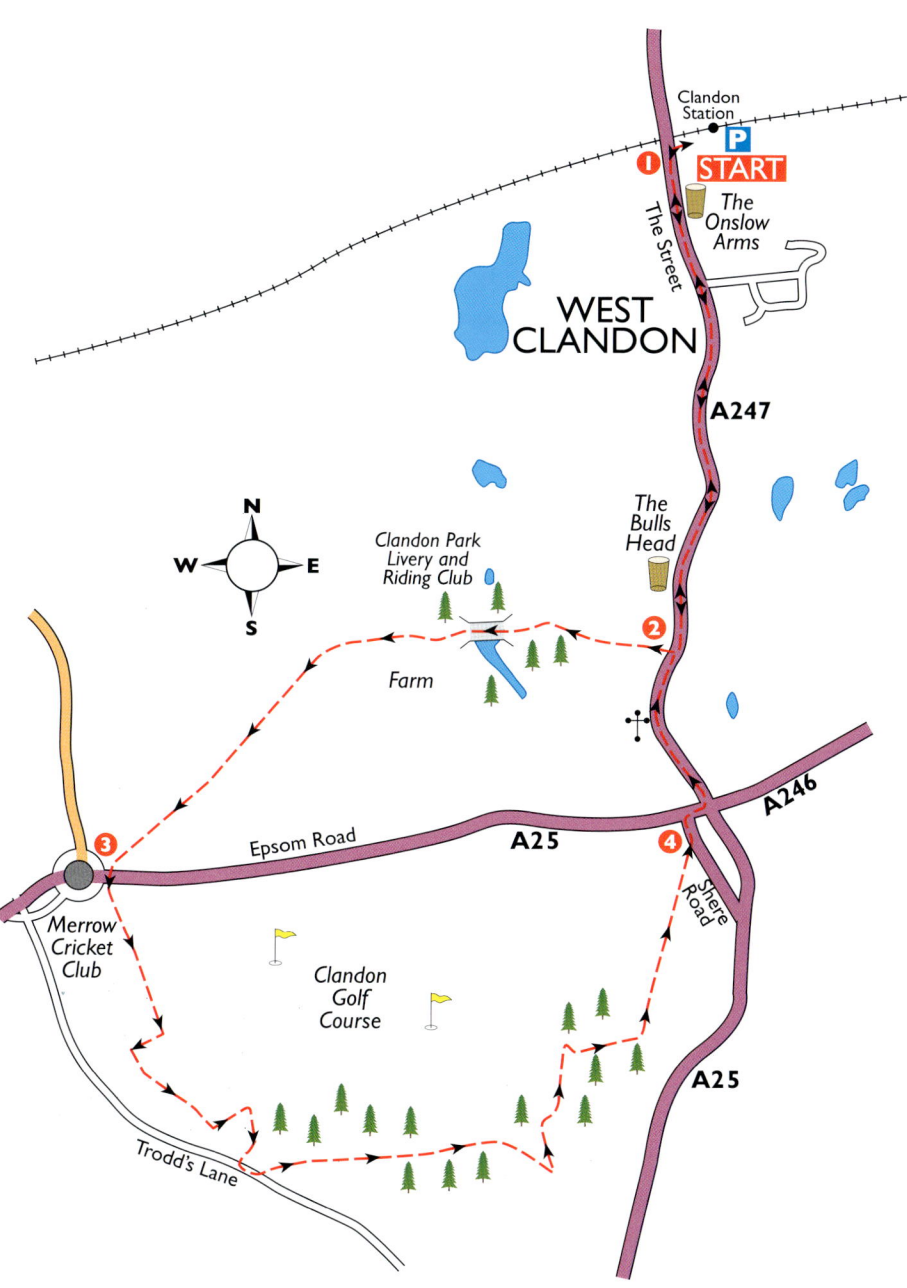

Surrey Pub Walks

be horses in the field on the right as you are walking near to **Clandon Park Livery and Riding Club**. There is a low gate at the end of the path, which you will have to climb over so take care. Next, follow a long path that borders two fields and takes you down towards the main **Epsom Road** and the ornate gold entrance gate.

❸ Be careful crossing the busy road and then head up the track opposite towards **Merrow Cricket Club**. Follow the path in between the cricket club and the sports club. When you get to the end of the path, keep ahead with **Clandon Golf course** to your left. The course is popular all year round as its geological make-up allows it to drain rain away brilliantly. Follow the path round to the right as it skirts the edge of the course. Needless

West Clandon 6

to say, take care if there are any golfers nearby. Turn left again, and then right heading into the woods. Shortly you will emerge from the woods onto **Trodd's Lane** which you should cross with care. Turn left and walk along the verge for a few metres, then be careful when you cross back over onto the golf course. Cross over in front of the tee box and down a path in between a wood and the course. When you reach a wide fairway of a downhill golf hole, stop and look up right to see if there are any golfers about to hit their balls down towards the hole. Make sure they see you before you put your hand up to ask to cross. If they have given you the go ahead, cross and soak up the great view to your left from this **Merrow Downs** area. Keep ahead down a long path in the woods, keeping parallel with the course, then head right through **Wildwood** towards some houses. Turn left when you reach the houses and head left down a stunning tree-lined path. This takes you all the way to the busy **Shere Road** where you turn left to a complicated road junction.

4 Cross over the double junction. There are no pedestrian crossings, so take care. Turn right and then immediately left to reach **The Street**. Keep going along **The Street** until you reach the **Onslow Arms** with the station car park beyond.

Places of Interest Nearby

West Clandon is known primarily for being surrounded by **Clandon Park**, a 1000-acre agricultural estate rebuilt in the 18th century that is the seat of the Earl of Onslow – one of the largest private landowners in Surrey. Clandon Park is a Palladian architecture mansion run by the National Trust, which was largely destroyed by a fire in April 2015 and is undergoing extensive renovation.
⊕ www.nationaltrust.org.uk/visit/surrey/clandon-park

Walk 7
GUILDFORD

Distance: 3½ miles (5.4 km)

Start: Guildford railway station, Station Approach, Guildford, GU1 4UT.

How to get there: Guildford is easy enough to get to via the A3 from the east and west, and several roads from the north like Worplesdon Road and Portsmouth Road to the south. There is an excellent South Western Railway service operating from London Waterloo, while regular buses are also available.

Parking: Park at the station car park.

Map: OS Explorer 145: Guildford & Farnham.
Grid Ref: SU991497.

This route rises up gradually through Surrey's striking county town via two very different but fun pubs before taking you back

Guildford 7

down past Guildford Castle to the final stop where you can relax with a drink overlooking the River Wey.

THE PUB **THE DRUMMOND** prides itself on providing great hospitality and seasonal menus that reflect the best of local produce They have an annual Craft Beer Residency and limited-edition beers on tap.
🌐 www.thedrummondguildford.co.uk ☎ 01483 579395.

THE PUB **THE ROYAL OAK** is believed to have once been part of the rectory for Holy Trinity Church whose history goes back to before local records began. Small in stature, but big on atmosphere, this dog-friendly pub has a cosy fireplace indoors and a nice beer garden to the rear.
🌐 www.royaloakguildford.co.uk ☎ 01483 457144.

THE PUB **THE WEYSIDE** is a scenic pub overlooking the River Wey that provides a fitting final stop on this Guildford adventure, especially during the sunnier months when the outdoor tables are buzzing with life and the river is teeming with wildlife.
🌐 www.theweyside.co.uk ☎ 01483 568024.

The Walk

❶ Head left out of the train station and bear right down **Station Approach**, then cross over onto the other side of **Walnut Tree Close** and take the small footbridge that goes over the **River Wey**. At the end of that, turn right into **Bedford Road** and head up to the **A322/Onslow Street**. Turn left onto the pavement and follow the main road until the roundabout when you keep left onto **Woodbridge Road** until you see the **Drummond** next to **Andertons Music Co** on the opposite side of the road. Cross over and enjoy your first stop of the walk then, head right out of the pub (or keep straight on if you haven't stopped) and take the first right up **Drummond Road**, then turn right along **Park Road** to reach the main **Stoke Road** by the **Stoke pub**. Cross over onto the other side and turn left up **Stoke Road** to **Nightingale Road**.

❷ Turn right and pass **Stoke Park** and the **Sensory Garden**. When you reach the first building on the left, turn left into **Stoke Park**

Surrey Pub Walks

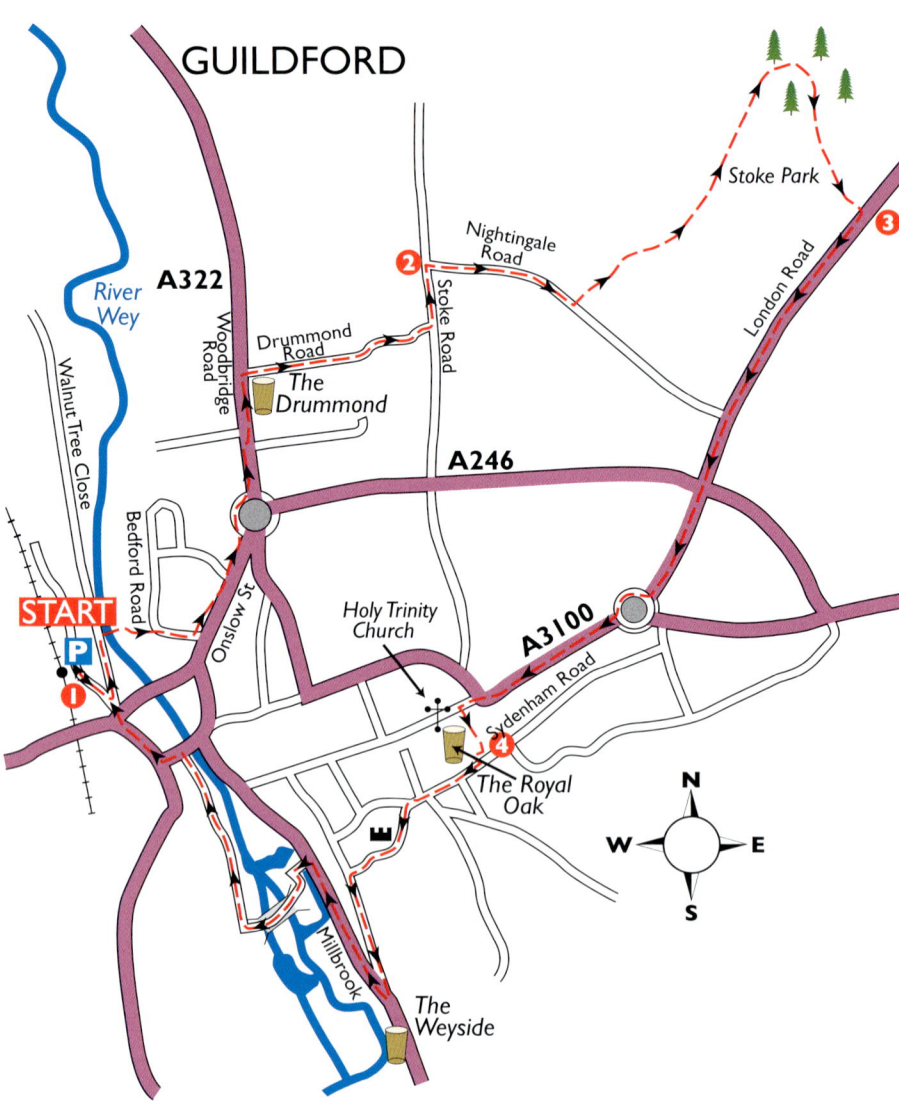

and along the long footpath that boasts pretty views back across the town. Stroll along this all the way until you see **Jubilee Wood**, which you head into. Turn right back through the wood and out the other side following the footpath that takes you back up the hill.

Guildford 7

3 When you reach the **A3100/London Road**, turn right onto the pavement and follow that all the way past the historic **Tank Traps** by **London Road Railway Station** and **G Live entertainment venue** that sits at the top of the **High Street**. Cross over onto the other side of the **High Street** and amble down past the intriguing architecture of the **Royal Grammar School Guildford** building all the way to the **Holy Trinity Church**. Turn left up the narrow **Trinity Churchyard** and follow it around to the right to locate the **Royal Oak** and the second stop, where you can rest up and revel in the cosy charm of another historic building.

4 When you've recharged, exit through the back of the pub up onto **Sydenham Road** and turn right to where it meets **Castle Street**, which is where you turn left into the **Guildford Castle** grounds. You can take time to explore these or simply follow the footpath in between the castle and **Castle Green Bowling Club** above that leads you down to **Quarry Street** below. Turn left at the bottom

Surrey Pub Walks

and follow it down with **Castle Cliffe Gardens** above to your left until you reach the main road at the bottom. Cross over here and turn left towards the **Weyside** where you can hopefully soak up the sun outdoors overlooking the **River Wey** or hunker down inside for the final stop on this walk. Once done, head left out of the pub and back up **Millbrook** until you reach a small road on your left that feeds you around the left of the **Yvonne Arnaud Theatre**. Cross over another River Wey footbridge into **Millmead** where you turn right past the **Britannia pub**, **Westnye Gardens** to your left and the **White House pub** to your right, up to where the road bears left. Head down onto the river footpath and meander down under **Onslow Street** above. Just after, turn left up the road that hugs the office building back to the **A322**. Take care crossing the road and then head back up towards **Guildford railway station**.

Places of Interest Nearby

Guildford High Street, with its Grade I-listed facades, feels rather like a stage set. It's always worth lingering for a while if you can. From here it's a short distance to the town's impressive **Norman castle**, where you can climb to the top of the **Great Tower** for 360-degree views of the town and surrounding countryside. Within the grounds you'll also find **Guildford Museum**, the perfect place to learn all about the town's rich history, from the Roman and Saxon periods right up to the modern era. ⊕ www.guildford.gov.uk.

Walk 8
SHERE

Distance: 3½ miles (5.6 km)

Start: Shere Car Park, London Lane, Shere, GU5 9HF.

How to get there: Shere is just off the A25 that runs between Dorking to the east and Guildford to the west. Gomshall railway station is four minutes away, while the 22, 25 and 32 buses are regular from the east, west and south.

Parking: Park in the village car park just off Upper Street.

Map: OS Explorer 145: Guildford & Farnham.
Grid Ref: TQ073479.

Take a stroll through one of the prettiest parts of the Surrey Hills AONB, on an undulating jaunt that will reward you with awe-inspiring views as well as a fine pub at the end. The picture-perfect village of Shere is well known to Hollywood location scouts thanks to its charming buildings and the idyllic River Tillingbourne.

Surrey Pub Walks

THE PUB

THE WILLIAM BRAY is a blissful pub that boasts a terrace, a conservatory and a beautifully decorated dining room. Their main menu revolves around fresh seasonal produce, while they also offer homemade cakes and pastries if you want a shorter coffee stop.
🌐 www.thebray.net/reserve-a-table ☎ 01483 202275.

The Walk

❶ Head out of **Shere Car Park**, cross **Upper Street**, and turn right down **Middle Street** opposite towards the central part of the village with its cosy cluster of shops and restaurants. When you get to the bridge going over the **River Tillingbourne**, turn right down **Lower Street** passing some charming houses. When you reach the end of the road, do not cross the river again, but

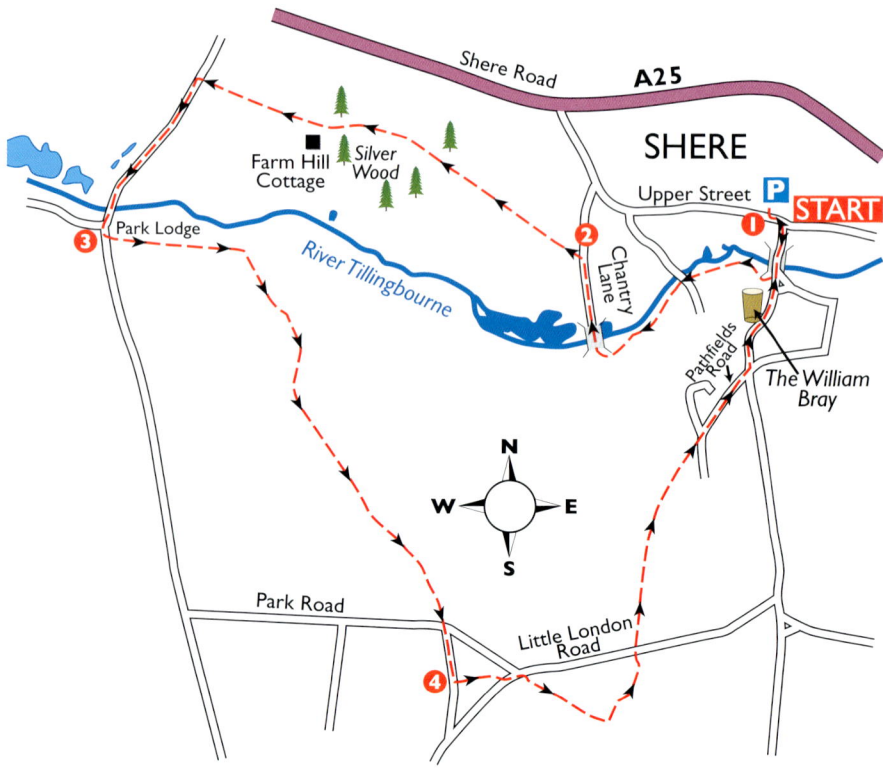

Shere 8

instead continue over onto **Lime Walk footpath**. Then bear right along another path that takes you to the bridge over the river just past the sluice. Turn right up **Chantry Lane** and keep watch for a footpath on the left up through the woods.

2 Head uphill until you get to a gate at the top. Continue along the footpath with the field on your right until you reach another gate that leads into **Silver Wood**. Rest a moment to take in the stunning views back across to Juniper Hill, Albury Downs and Combe Bottom, then stroll along the ridge line. Take care when heading downhill to another gate, which opens up to another large field which takes you past **Farm Hill Cottage** on your left and leads to **Sherbourne Catholic Apostolic Church**. Turn left at the **A248** road down a path that takes you past the church entrance and down to a bridge over the river. Bear left up **New Road** and immediately left again to reach the drive to the **Albury Park estate**.

3 Head up past **Park Lodge** and, when the drive forks, keep right above the higher road across a grassy hill to the gate at the entrance of the **Albury Park woods**. Be careful in slippery weather when you head uphill before it flattens out into a long footpath through a spellbinding stretch of woods. Keep following the path through the woods which eventually takes you down to **South Lodge** on your right and **Park Road**. Here you cross over and head down the path opposite towards a beautiful house.

4 Take the grassy footpath to the left which takes you to **Little London Road**. Cross with care and head left towards a big gate that lies at the junction with **Park Road**. Go through the gate and amble along a bridleway that allows you a lovely view of the trains to your right as you approach the railway crossing. Just before it, turn left along the bridleway that leads to **Little London Road** again. Watch out for traffic, then go straight over, heading down a bridleway that leads into a mysterious hollow in between **Shere Heath** and **The Plantation**. Keep ahead and then bear right at a forked marker down the bridleway to the **Rydings** where you can sometimes pick up duck eggs from outside a local farm. This takes you into **Pathfields road** and

Surrey Pub Walks

through a housing estate back to **Shere Lane**. Turn left, and then follow the lane to the **William Bray** where you can enjoy a well-earned break for food and drink. Head back up **Middle Street**, left up **Upper Street** and then immediately right to return to the car park.

Places of Interest Nearby

Shere is set in the wooded Vale of Holmesdale between the North Downs and Greensand Ridge. The area's history includes sheep-stealers, smugglers and poachers who found a refuge in the remote hills. It boasts a cluster of charming shops and buildings and is better known in more recent times as being a popular filming location for romantic comedies such as *The Holiday* starring Kate Winslet and Jude Law. If you're here on a weekend you might get lucky and find the little **village museum** open. www.sheremuseum.co.uk

Walk 9
Wonersh

Distance: 3 miles (5 km)

Start: The Grantley Arms, The Street, Wonersh, GU5 0PE.

How to get there: The Grantley Arms is located 15 minutes south of the A3 through Guildford, down the A281 and B2128 with Cranleigh Road to the east and The Street to the west. The nearest railway station is Shalford to the north five minutes away by taxi that passes between Reading and Redhill, while you can also access it using the 53 and 63 buses.

Parking: Park at the pub if visiting or roadside along The Street.

Map: OS Explorer 145: Guildford & Farnham.
Grid Ref: TQ017452.

This is a gem of a walk in a beautiful part of Surrey, halfway between Guildford and Cranleigh, which takes you around the village and along the Wey and Arun canal before circling up and

43

Surrey Pub Walks

over Chinthurst Hill. Wallow in the stunning views all around from over 100 metres above sea level, before you return to the award-winning pub.

Note: wear long trousers if walking in the summer months as some of the paths can be a bit overgrown with nettles.

THE PUB **THE GRANTLEY ARMS** is a classy, historic Young's pub in the heart of the village that prides itself on being a community hub. Timbered exteriors, open fires and hearty food are the order of the day – a quintessential country pub, and the perfect place to finish after a good walk.
⊕ www.thegrantleyarms.co.uk ☎ 01483 893351.

The Walk

❶ Head left out of the pub and stay on the left down **The Street**, then switch pavements to the other side at the historic **Wonersh House** and back again to the other side at **Wonersh Hollow**. Follow the road round to the left and across the beautiful **Wonersh Bridge** with lovely views on both sides.

❷ Turn right up **Eastwood Road**, then follow the bend round to the left and turn right up until you join the footpath. Walk along the path until you reach the canal then, when you see the **Wey & Arun Canal** sign, turn left on the tarmac path through the trees. When you reach **Tannery Lane** above, take the winding path to your right which brings you up onto **Tannery Lane** itself. Walk on the high pavement over **Drodges Close** and then listen out for traffic before crossing over **Chinthurst Lane** where you join the bridle path opposite that runs to the left of the gated equestrian centre.

❸ Wind your way up the sandy path to the top of the incline. You might encounter a boggy bit here, so take care until you reach a junction for the **Downs Link**. Take the first right, along the bridleway until you reach the junction with **The Tower** sign.

❹ Turn right, away from **Chinthurst Hill Car Park**, and head up the tricky path until you reach a choice of smooth path or steps. If you take the steps, then turn right at the top and follow

Wonersh

the path up the hill and more steps that deliver you out to a stunning view across to Wonersh and Blackheath where there is a bench for a well-deserved rest. After that, follow the path around to a gate and turn sharp right up another steep part up on to **Chinthurst Hill**. When you see steps on the left, head up over the heath to the tower. You are now at the top of **Chinthurst Hill** where you can drink in the amazing views that span across the Surrey Hills in all their beauty.

5 When you have taken a break, head left of the tower and down a steepish path. Pass through a gate, then join the road, turning right and heading down to the beautiful stone building that is

Wonersh

Chinthurst Hill Lodge. Being careful to listen out for traffic, bear left onto **Chinthurst Lane** and head underneath the trees. Keep ahead until you reach the junction with **Station Road** and **The Street** where you keep left along **The Street** and retrace your steps back to the pub.

Places of Interest Nearby

Wonersh has been home to a settlement since Anglo-Saxon times and contains three Conservation Areas and three architecturally listed churches. **Chinthurst Hill** – that rises majestically above the village – is managed by Surrey Wildlife Trust.

Just north of Wonersh you'll also find **Chilworth Gunpowder Mills**, founded by the East India Company in 1626. This is one of the earliest examples of a gunpowder mill – for a period in the 17th century, it was the only legal supplier of gunpowder in England to the King.

Walk 10

Godalming & Farncombe

Distance: 3 miles (4.8 km)

Start: Godalming Railway Station, Godalming, GU7 1EU.

How to get there: You can either take the train to Godalming railway station on South Western Railway, or park at the station car park. There are also regular buses such as the 46, 70, 71 and 72 taking you in most directions.

Parking: Park at Godalming Station Car Park or, if this is very busy try Mint Street Car Park or Mill Lane Car Park, at the west end of the High Street.

Map: OS Explorer 145: Guildford & Farnham.
Grid Ref: SU966440.

Godalming & Farncombe 🔟

Ideal for all ages, this walk combines a pleasant mix of the vibrant Godalming town centre, the Lammas Lands floodplain meadows and an undulating journey around Farncombe. It also features two characterful pubs, all in a part of Surrey that sometimes gets overlooked thanks to its proximity to Guildford.

THE PUB — **THE CRICKETERS** in Farncombe boasts Fuller's awards and Cask Marque accreditation. It has an interesting history and is the type of homely, Surrey community pub that seems to be thriving again, thanks to a classy refurbishment and cracking selection of food and drink. There is plenty of outdoor seating to the back of the pub where you can catch the evening sun.
🌐 www.cricketersfarncombe.co.uk ☎ 01483 424860.

THE PUB — **THE STAR** in Godalming can justifiably claim to be one of the best pubs in Surrey – it's a regular Great British Pub of the Year finalist, a previous Godalming in Bloom winner, and with its eclectic selection of ciders and real ales, has been voted CAMRA Regional Cider Pub (Surrey & Hampshire) for a record-breaking eight years in a row. The folk, pizza and quiz nights are very popular, as is the buzzy garden.
🌐 www.starinngodalming.co.uk ☎ 01483 417717.

The Walk

❶ Once you emerge from **Godalming railway station**, turn right out of **Station Approach** into **Mill Lane** and follow that, over the river, and all the way up to where it meets **Station Road**. Turn right and then immediately left, which takes you to the top of the **High Street**. Wander down the length of it past a spirited mix of local and chain shops, cafés, pubs and restaurants until you bear left down into **Bridge Street**. Follow that past **Waitrose**, towards a roundabout and cross the small bridge.

❷ From the right-hand pavement dip down onto the footpath that runs along the left-hand side of the **River Wey**. Meander along this endearing footpath, which occasionally gets muddy after sustained rain. This stretches along the border of the **Lammas Lands** floodplain meadows which are the remains

Surrey Pub Walks

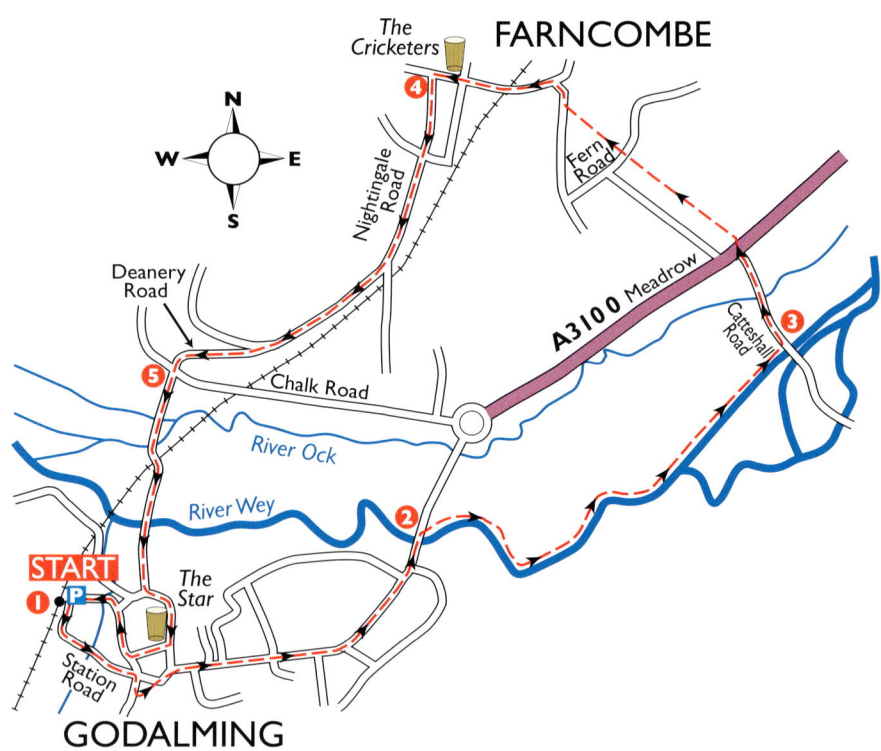

of a medieval field system. They cover 31.8 hectares and are recognised as a Site of Importance for Nature Conservation, an Area of High Archaeological Potential and an Area of Strategic Visual Importance thanks to 108 species of flowering plants, 227 invertebrates and six amber and 12 red-listed species of bird.

❸ After around ½ mile you will reach the **Farncombe Boat House**, where you turn left onto **Catteshall Road** and follow it over **Hell Ditch** until you reach **Meadrow**. Be careful crossing the road, then take the footpath directly opposite which brings you up to **Fern Road** where you cross over again and continue to **St John's Street**. Turn right, cross over the road and bear left into **Farncombe Street**. Follow that for around 200m up to the junction of **Nightingale Road**.

Godalming & Farncombe 10

4 Turn left until you reach the **Cricketers pub** where you can enjoy a well-earned drink or bite to eat and look back down to the **Lammas Lands**. Keep ahead along **Nightingale Road** to **Nightingale Cemetery** where you turn right at the fork along **Deanery Road**. This leads you down to the junction with **Chalk Road**.

5 Take care when crossing over into **Borough Road** and keep ahead until you cross over **Hell Ditch** again, with the floodplain extending back out to the left. Continue ahead and pass over the pretty, meandering **River Ock** and up past the **Phillips Memorial Cloister** – a charming Grade II listed Arts and Crafts building that is named after local Jack Phillips, the radio operator aboard the RMS *Titanic*, and is part of the **Phillips Memorial Park**. Bear left up into historically charged **Church Street** where you can enjoy a deserved rest with a visit to the Star, one of Surrey's finest pubs. Turn right down **Mint Street** and right again to **Station Road** which takes you back to the station.

Surrey Pub Walks

Places of Interest Nearby

Farncombe is part of one of the five wards that make up Godalming, and it rises up from the **Farncombe Boat House** on the River Wey to Charterhouse school on the hill above. Day boats are available for hire at Farncombe Boat House, giving you a chance to experience the canals that helped drive prosperity here in years gone by. ⊕ farncombeboats.co.uk

A couple of miles to the south is **Winkworth Arboretum**. This tranquil hillside spot with stunning year-round displays was created by Dr Wilfrid Fox in the early 20th century and is now looked after by the National Trust. ⊕ www.nationaltrust.org.uk/visit/surrey/winkworth-arboretum

Walk 11
Chiddingfold

Distance: 3 miles (5 km)

Start: The Crown Inn, The Green, Petworth Road, Chiddingfold GU8 4TX.

How to get there: The Crown Inn is located on the A283 between Fisherstreet to the south and North Bridge to the north with access to the east also available via Pickhurst Road to the southeast, Pockford Road to the east and country lanes to the west. There is parking around the green. Even though there are no train stations in the immediate vicinity, bus routes operate from Guildford and Godalming to the north down to Haslemere in the south.

Parking: Park at the pub if visiting or roadside along The Green.

Map: OS Explorer OL33: Haslemere & Petersfield.
Grid Ref: SU960353.

53

Surrey Pub Walks

This charming walk is perfect to build up an appetite for lunch or dinner, with just one sizeable elevation to deal with in an enchanting area of Surrey often missed as people shuttle between Guildford and Haslemere. The hour-long walk takes in rolling fields and fascinating woodland such as Smithers Land Hanger. The route can get very muddy after rain so worth picking a dry day.

THE PUB **THE CROWN INN** is one of the oldest inns in England and is thought to have been constructed as a rest house for Cistercian monks on their pilgrimage from Winchester to the shrine of Thomas Becket in Canterbury. Original deeds from 1383 hang above the impressive stone fireplace, while elsewhere it's all oak beams, stained-glass windows, creaking floorboards and vintage furniture.
🌐 www.thecrownchiddingfold.com   ☎ 01428 682255.

The Walk

① With your back to **The Crown Inn**, turn left down **Petworth Road** and past the butchers. Pass **Turners Mead** road and once the houses peter out on the left, there is a footpath that

Chiddingfold 11

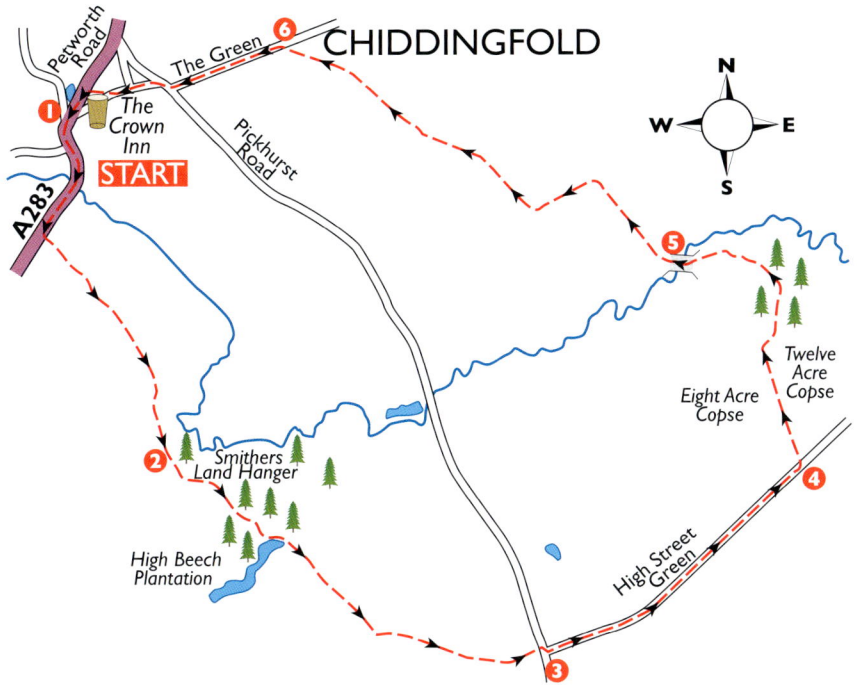

cuts left behind them. Take this and head to a gate where you then cross a field. Follow the slope down until you see some steps on the right at the bottom. Walk up them and head left along the path. You will reach another gate, which goes across some water.

2 Head up into the pretty woods then keep ahead staying as close to the field line as possible. You will eventually reach a large swing gate, which you go through. Next, head left down a series of steep steps and please be extra careful here. There is a pond at the bottom where you can catch your breath right where **Smithers Land Hanger** and **High Beech Plantation** border each other. Head across the bridge and up to the top where you will see another field. Follow the path on a slight slope that borders the field to the left and woods to the right. You will reach a stile by the entrance to a house, which you go over. Head left down the drive, then across the main road into **High Street Green**.

Surrey Pub Walks

3 Follow the road past **Timbers Chase** on your left until you reach cottages on your right.

4 Turn left into the footpath that runs between **Eight Acre Copse** and **Twelve Acre Copse**. There is an easier path to the left of the main vehicular path that heads into the woods, if footing is easier there. When you reach the point where another path joins on the right, head down a little bit until you see the electricity pylons around you, then follow the path left alongside them. You will reach a very steep part next, with steep steps, where it is easier to go down sideways, particularly in damp conditions. Turn left at the bottom down a path that takes you to a bridge over the water.

5 Go left at the bridge, then head right uphill along the field with the woods on your right. Bear left at the top along the hedgerow

Chiddingfold

and, a few hundred metres along, look for an opening. Head through the opening and over the next field that leads you to a gap in the tree line. Cross the next field, through a small copse and over into another field. You will get to another gate. Head through that and over the last stretch of grass until you reach the **Pockford Road gate**.

6 Climb over the stile and turn left down towards the village, then bear right at **Pickhurst Road**. Turn left at **The Green** and follow the path back down towards **The Crown Inn** where you can enjoy a well-earned rest.

Places of Interest Nearby

Here's something to keep in mind while you explore this little corner of Surrey: **Chiddingfold** is famous for its glass making, with no fewer than 11 glass works on the green during the reign of Queen Elizabeth I. John de Alemaygne supplied large quantities of glass in 1352 for St Stephen's Chapel at Westminster with St George's Chapel, Windsor, also benefiting from broad sheet glass made in the village near to **Chiddingfold Forest**.

Walk 12
SURBITON & KINGSTON

Distance: 3 miles (5 km)

Start: Surbiton Railway Station, Victoria Road, Surbiton, KT6 4PE.

How to get there: Surbiton is easy to get to quickly by train from London Waterloo to the north east in 20-30 minutes or from Basingstoke, Guildford, Portsmouth and Woking. You can also access it easily using a number of buses from all directions such as the 281, 465, K1 and K2 routes, while it is just off the Tolworth junction of the A3 by car or taxi, or use the A307 to the west, Hook Road to the south or A240 to the east.

Parking: Park at Surbiton Railway Station car park.

Map: OS Explorer 161: London South. **Grid Ref:** TQ180672.

Surbiton & Kingston 12

Less than half an hour by train from the centre of London, this delightful stroll around Surbiton, Kingston and along the River Thames takes in a trio of pubs that offer quality gastro food and drink, with the atmosphere to match. Whether you only have a couple of hours or the whole afternoon and evening, this makes for a different, but equally worthwhile outing.

THE PUB — **THE SPRING GROVE** in Kingston Upon Thames is nestled in the area between Surbiton and Kingston town centres. The Young's pub prides itself on their cask-conditioned ales, craft beer, award-winning wines and premium spirits. A menu featuring seasonal produce, live sport and their sprawling "secret" beer garden are other standout attractions.
⊕ www.thespringgrove.co.uk ☎ 020 8549 9507.

THE PUB — **THE ALBION,** also in Kingston Upon Thames, has a huge range of pale ales, lagers and rich stouts alongside hearty food including homemade burgers, smoked meats and roasts. The all-weather garden is a fab space.
⊕ www.thealbionkingston.com ☎ 020 8541 1691.

THE PUB — **THE ANTELOPE** in Surbiton is where the Big Smoke Brew Co originated, until the brewery side of the business became so big that they had to move to larger premises. A hugely admired pub in this part of Surrey, it offers a wide range of real ales, ciders and keg beers as well as home-cooked food and a lively atmosphere with fun music.
⊕ www.theantelope.co.uk ☎ 020 8399 5565.

The Walk

❶ Come out of the main entrance to **Surbiton station**, head across the roundabout towards **Waitrose** and follow **Claremont Road** down to the junction of **Maple Road**. Turn right and walk along **Maple Road** to the main junction and traffic lights. Cross over and keep ahead into **Beaufort Road**. Turn left at the junction with **Cranes Park** which still retains the Beaufort Road name until you get to where it meets **Grove Lane**. Cross over at the roundabout into **Bloomfield Road** and stay on the right-hand side to arrive at the **Spring Grove** and your first chance to take a food or drink stop.

Surrey Pub Walks

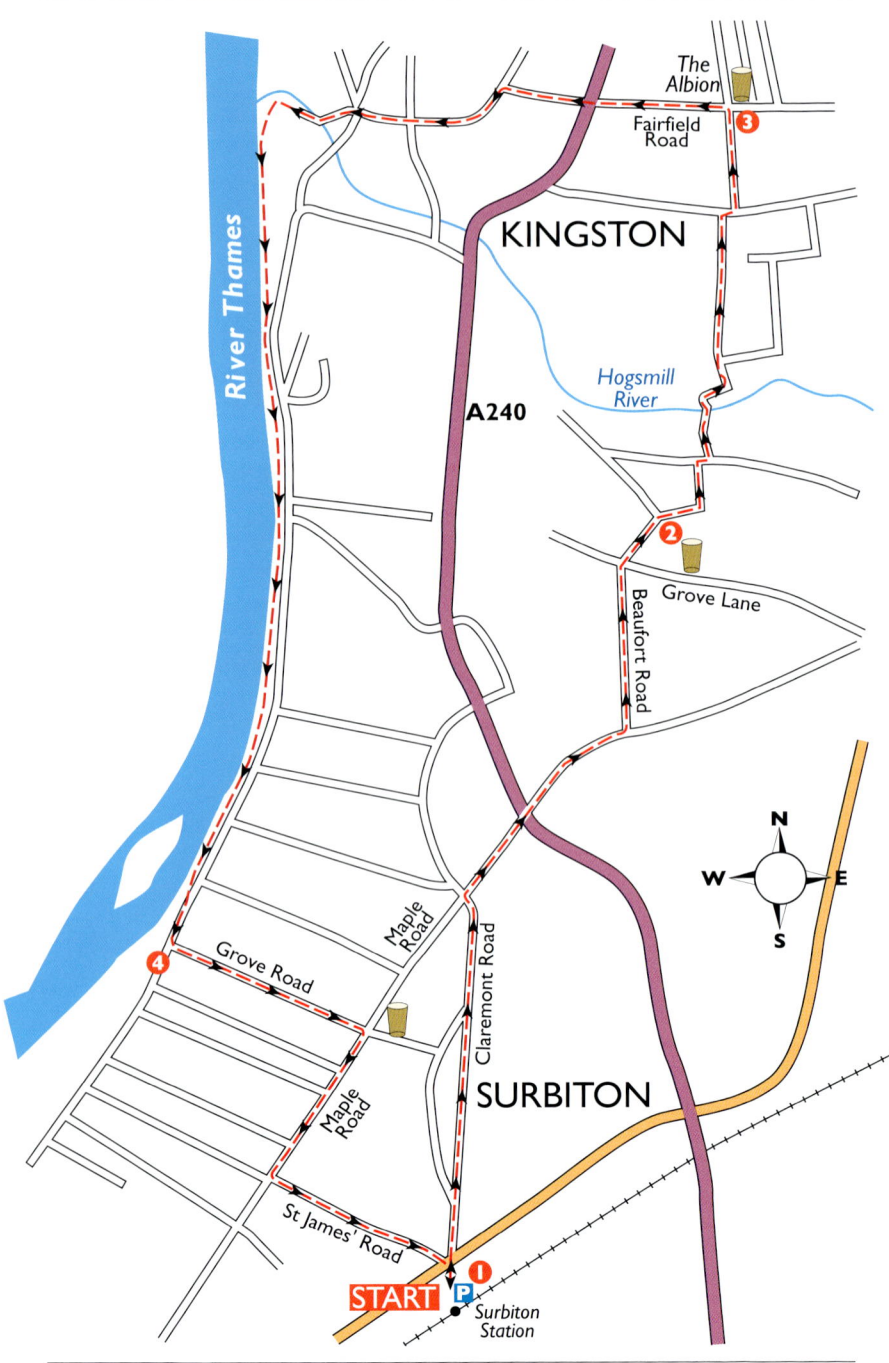

Surbiton & Kingston 12

2 Keep ahead down **Bloomfield Road** then cross over and turn left up a road and then a footpath that takes you to **Portland Road**. Cross over and keep ahead down **Three Bridges Path** opposite that crosses the **Hogsmill River** and takes you past **Kingston School of Art** and into **Mill Street**. Turn left and stroll up the length of the road, then cross over **Fairfield South** into **Fairfield Recreation Ground** and the footpath that delivers you out to the **Albion** on **Fairfield Road**.

3 Turn left along **Fairfield Road** (or right out of the pub if you've visited) and cross over the traffic lights at **Wheatfield Way** into **Lady Booth Road** and the heart of Kingston town centre. At the bottom of **Lady Booth Road**, turn left down **Eden Street** and follow that around until you reach the junction of **Market Place**. Head into **Market Place** and down a footpath on your left that has a buzzing selection of cafés, bars and restaurants, which delivers you out alongside the **Hogsmill River**. Turn right up

Surrey Pub Walks

Charter Quay, then turn left down to **Riverside Walk**. This is a lovely ¾-mile stretch along the **River Thames** that goes all the way down to **Raven's Ait** that sits in the middle of the river. Here you leave the riverside path and come to **Portsmouth Road**.

❹ Cross at the pedestrian crossing, turn right and then left up **Grove Road** to the junction of **Maple Road** and the **Grove pub**. Turn right down **Maple Road** until you reach the final stop of the **Antelope**, where you can indulge in their enviable beer and cider selection. Keep walking along **Maple Road** for a short distance and then take the first left onto **St James' Road** back up to the station.

Places of Interest Nearby

If you can time your visit to coincide with the monthly **Surbiton Farmers' Market** on Maple Road, so much the better. This community event, which brings together 26 farmers and producers selling fresh produce and speciality foods, takes place on the third Saturday of each month. www.surbitonfarmersmarket.co.uk

Down the road in **Kingston**, consider making some extra time to explore the riverside walk, a delightful public promenade that follows a visually arresting mile-long stretch of the **Thames**.

Walk 13
Epsom Common

Distance: 2¼ miles (3.6 km)

Start: The Jolly Coopers, 84 Wheelers Lane, Epsom, KT18 7SD.

How to get there: The Jolly Coopers is accessible off the B280/ Christ Church Road that runs from the back of Epsom to the east, Chessington to the north and Oxshott to the west. Once you turn off the B280, head down Stamford Green Road until you get to Wheelers Lane on your left and the pub. Epsom train station is just 15 minutes' walk away, while the E10 bus runs along the B280 into Epsom if you prefer to get off at the nearby Christ Church stop.

Parking: Park at the pub if visiting or roadside along Wheelers Lane.

Map: OS Explorer 161: London South. **Grid Ref:** TQ198604.

Surrey Pub Walks

This mostly flat, sedate walk is fairly short and suitable for all ages, whether you want to build up an appetite or stretch the legs in an area of Surrey steeped in history. It includes a stop at one of the town's oldest pubs.

THE PUB **THE JOLLY COOPERS** is a pub for all seasons; the paved and partly covered garden area is perfect in the summer months, while the wood-burning stove and mottled windows bring the winter cosiness. They have their own microbrewery in an outbuilding under the name of Fuzzchat. A CAMRA (Campaign for Real Ale) favourite, the brewery is the first new one in Epsom for nearly 100 years and provides beers for the pub itself as well as the surrounding area. Food is seasonal and locally sourced.
🌐 www.jollycoopers.co.uk ☎ 01372 723222.

❶ The Walk

From the pub head back to **Stamford Green Road** and turn left to reach **Lewins Road**. Turn right and, at the end, keep ahead up **Summers Gate** footpath for around ¼ mile. At the road turn right, and then right again back onto a footpath.

Epsom Common 13

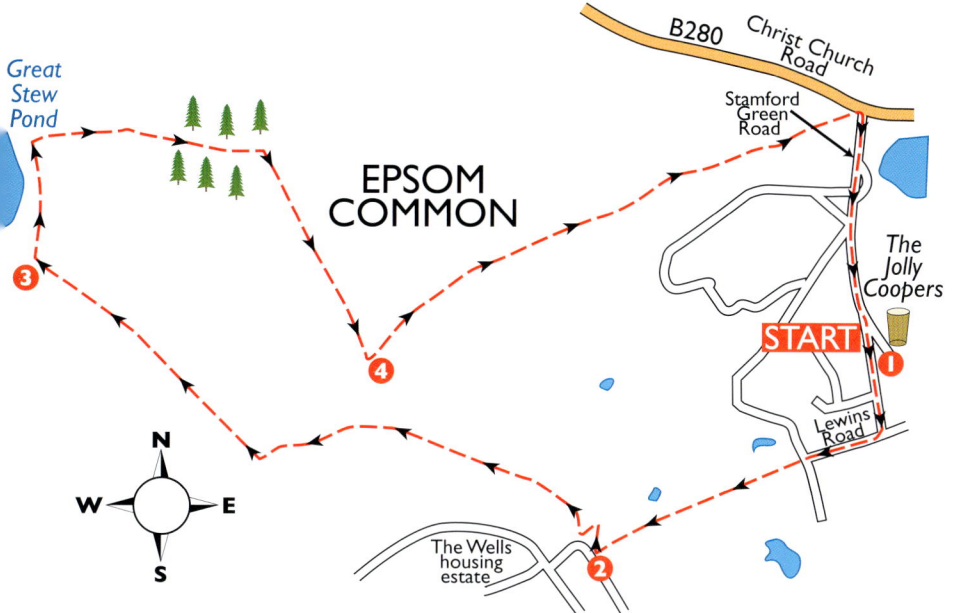

2 Follow the path round to the left, skirting the edge of The Wells housing estate and into **Epsom Common**. Amble downhill until you reach a bench on the right, where you turn right up a narrow (often muddy) track. If it is too muddy, then divert alongside it on the right over the grassland towards **Great Stew Pond**.

3 Just before the pond, head right over a plank across a stream onto a path where you can pause to take in the eclectic flora and fauna. Follow the path to the end, then turn right and go through the kissing gate. Head right, down a wide bridle path with three trees towering over either side. At the junction bear right onto another main path.

4 When you approach a confluence of paths, turn hard left and join a wider path. Keep ahead for around ½ mile, Stamford Green soon appears on your right, until you reach the B280 **Christ Church Road**. Turn right down **Stamford Green Road** to return to the pub.

Surrey Pub Walks

Places of Interest Nearby

Chessington World of Adventure is only a few minutes' drive away. Open all year round, it's home to a theme park, a zoo, hotels and glamping. www.chessington.com

Also, seeing as you're in this part of the world, it would make sense to see whether there's any racing on at the world-famous **Epsom Downs racecourse**. They regularly have evening racing in the summer, which would make a great way to finish off your day. www.thejockeyclub.co.uk

Walk 14
HEADLEY

Distance: 4 miles (6.4 km)

Start: Headley Heath Car Park (NT), Headley Common Road, Headley, KT18 6NN.

How to get there: Headley Heath Car Park is located about 11 minutes' drive south from Junction 9 of the M25 via the A24, while you can also access it from the north by Tilley Lane and B2033 from the south. It is also 10 minutes by taxi from Leatherhead railway station to the north, which shuttles between London, Dorking, Horsham and Guildford, and six minutes from Betchworth railway station to the south served by Great Western Railway. The 21 bus between Dorking and Epsom also stops nearby.

Parking: Park in the main car park which is operated by the National Trust.

Map: OS Explorer 146: Dorking, Box Hill & Reigate.
Grid Ref: TQ205538.

Surrey Pub Walks

Boasting some of the most magical views in this book, this is a thorough workout, over the first half especially. It can get boggy, so I recommend doing it in sunnier weather if possible. The route takes in parts of easy-on-the-eye Headley Heath, Mickleham Downs and Nower Wood, while the Cock Inn is a popular country pub.

THE PUB — **THE COCK INN** is popular with foodies, cyclists and ramblers, with a menu that focuses on seasonal, local produce, and plenty of options for children and gluten-free diners. They have an extensive selection of local real ales, lagers and ciders from the likes of Hogs Back Brewery and Tilford Brewery.
🌐 www.cockinnheadley.co.uk ☎ 01372 377258.

The Walk

❶ With your back to the road bear left out of the car park down towards the **Heath**. Head through a gate with 'cattle grazing' warnings and down towards a picturesque pond on the left. Carry straight on over the grass down towards the ridge line at **Ranmore Vista** with stunning views back left. Take care going down a steepish, rocky path that feeds down into a muddy path at the bottom.

❷ Keep ahead passing steps to your left and right and head up a steep, snaking path that is rocky with tree roots. At the top, turn right down a narrow path that borders a house with logs piled up either side. Wind down the narrow path with a field and then **Cockshot Cottage** on your left towards **Lodgebottom Road** and a car park. Listen for traffic before walking across, then bear left along the pretty footpath on the high side of the road on the edge of the wood.

❸ With **Cockshot Wood** on your right, turn

68

Headley 14

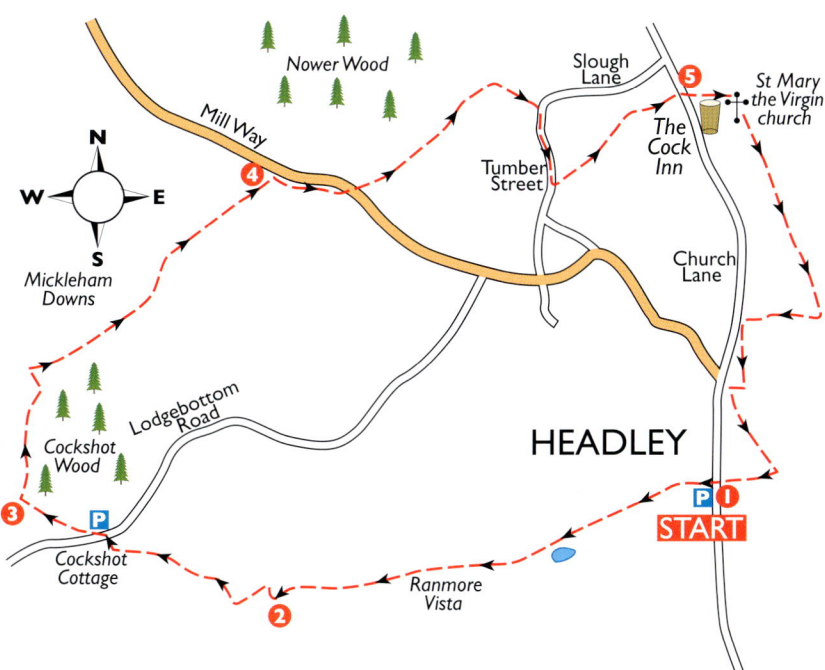

right to head up the steep path through the moss-covered trees. Keep following the path until you reach the top, where **Mickleham Downs** spreads out to your left. Turn right towards **Nower Wood** along a bridle path which you follow for just over ¼ mile.

4 When you get to **Mill Way** and a parking area, turn right along the path that runs parallel to the road. In 300m cross over carefully and join a path on your left that runs towards **Headley**. If the main path is very muddy, it is easy to walk in the woods alongside it by the fields. In ¼ mile the path curves to the right, past some houses, to meet a road where **Slough Lane** turns into **Tumber Street**. Turn right down the hill past some houses until you reach a gate on your left. Once through the gate, make your way up the narrow path past some stables and houses, then bear right up a steep incline through a gate that takes you back to **Church Lane** and the **Cock Inn**.

Surrey Pub Walks

Dr Neil Clifton

5 Once you have replenished some energy, go round to the back of the pub and pass through the churchyard of **St Mary the Virgin church** towards the back gate. Turn right down a bridle path and keep straight on for just under ½ mile through kissing gates and over fields until you get to a path on the right that borders **Webbs Farm**. Do not be alarmed by what appears to be paintball gunfire from the woods on your left during this stretch. Amble up the bridle path to **Church Lane** where you turn left following the path behind the edge of the cricket green, then turn right at the back of the cricket pavilion and cross the road to return to the car park.

Places of Interest Nearby

Headley Heath is a beautiful mix of open heathland, woodland and chalk downland in Surrey's North Downs, part of the beguiling Surrey Hills AONB.

Just a 15-minute drive away you'll find the National Trust site of **Polesden Lacey**, a 1600-acre site with sprawling gardens and an elegant Edwardian mansion, the onetime home of socialite Margaret Greville.
www.nationaltrust.org.uk/visit/surrey/polesden-lacey

Walk 15
Leigh

Distance: 2¾ miles (4.4 km)

Start: The Plough, Church Road, Leigh, RH2 8NJ.

How to get there: The Plough is around 15 minutes' drive from the A24 to the west and M25 to the north, and 20 minutes from the M23 to the east with Smalls Hill Road feeding into it from the south, Flanchford Road from the east, Snowerhill Road from the north and Bunce Common Road from the west. You can reach it easily enough by taxi with a 10-minute drive from Betchworth, Holmwood and Reigate railway stations, while the 22 bus passes by fairly regularly as well as occasional 50, 433 and 522 Mole Valley Villager buses.

Parking: Park at the pub if visiting, or roadside in the small lay-by opposite the church.

Map: OS Explorer 146: Dorking, Box Hill & Reigate.
Grid Ref: TQ223469.

Surrey Pub Walks

A gentle walk that's perfect for a family outing before you tuck into hearty food and drink at the Plough overlooking the village green. A great chance to stretch your legs properly, whether clambering over stiles, strolling through fields or crossing the streams that dot the walk.

THE PUB — **THE PLOUGH** dates back to the late 14th century, with a low-beamed lounge bar and cosy restaurant that serves up filling home-cooked food and delicious ice cream from nearby St Joan's Farm Dairy. Features plenty of outside seating in the pretty patio garden or at the front under the giant umbrella. Dog friendly.
⊕ www.theploughleigh.co.uk ☎ 01306 611348.

The Walk

❶ Head left from the **Plough** along **Church Road** and past the church. When the road starts bearing left, cross over and head into the field on the right. Stroll across the clear path through the middle of the field, with **Leigh Place** on your left, until

Leigh 15

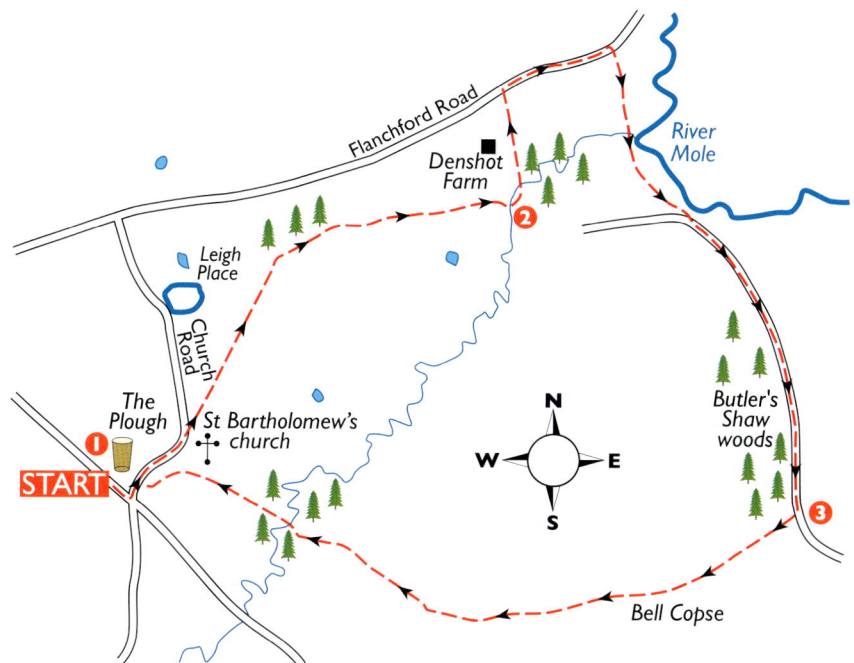

you reach some trees on the other side. Bear right alongside the stream for around ½ mile until you reach the woods at the back of **Denshot Farm**.

❷ Turn left here, keeping the farm on your left-hand side, until you reach **Flanchford Road**. Watch out for traffic and turn right past a small road until you reach a stile on your right. Cross the stile and follow the footpath on the left that hugs the **River Mole**. Keep ahead when it joins a lane for a further ½ mile, passing the **Coach House**, **Burys Court** and **Butler's Shaw woods** on your right.

❸ Turn right at the end of the woods and follow the footpath past **Bell Copse** on your left until you reach a stile on your right, which you need to climb over. Turn left, taking the middle footpath between the two fields until you reach another wooded area, then cross over the stream and follow the footpath over one more field into the trees at the back of the churchyard.

Surrey Pub Walks

Stay left of the church and head across the green back to the pub.

Places of Interest Nearby

A few miles to the north of Leigh you'll find **Buckland Park Lake**, a watersports lagoon that's home to The Surrey Hills Adventure Company, who run stand-up paddle boarding and open-water swimming sessions. ⊕ bucklandparklake.co.uk

Also nearby is **Reigate Fort**, an atmospheric Victorian-era structure looked after by the National Trust that sits at the top of Reigate Hill. Originally constructed to help defend London from invasion by the French, it has exceptional views over the surrounding countryside.

Walk 16
COLDHARBOUR

Distance: 3½ miles (5.5 km)

Start: The Plough Inn, Abinger Rd, Coldharbour, RH5 6HD.

How to get there: The Plough Inn is a tricky pub to get to, however it is well worth the journey whether you are coming from Dorking to the north via Coldharbour Lane or from the east via the A24 and country lanes. You can also access it from the south via Ockley and west via Leith Hill through country lanes and Abinger Road respectively. Holmwood to the east is the nearest train station, while the 433 and 50 buses pass by with long journeys from Dorking.

Parking: Park at the pub but please ask permission from the landlord before leaving your car.

Map: OS Explorer 146: Dorking, Box Hill & Reigate.
Grid Ref: TQ151441.

A contender for one of the most beautiful walks in Surrey, this captivating route provides some of the best views in the

Surrey Pub Walks

county as you pass through parts of Coldharbour Common, Duke's Warren, Milton Gore and Waterden Wood. Parking is at a premium at the pub, so it is wise to undertake the walk outside peak hours.

THE PUB

THE PLOUGH INN is a favourite with walkers, tourists and bikers, and it's easy to see why. Traditional food is served using in-season game such as venison, pheasant, partridge and rabbit, as well as locally foraged mushrooms. Unsurprisingly, they are previous winners of *Surrey Life* awards for best local menu. The pub has its own microbrewery on site, as well as a shop and six individually furnished bedrooms.
⊕ www.ploughinn.com ☎ 01306 711793.

The Walk

❶ Cross the road from the **Plough Inn** and head left up the long, steep track that borders **Coldharbour Common**. In ¼ mile you reach **Coldharbour Cricket Club** ground where you bear right then keep ahead alongside the ground, past the gate and along the path to another gate. Follow the path down a small descent.

❷ At the junction, turn sharp right back along the ridge where beautiful views across the countryside open up in all their glory.

Coldharbour 16

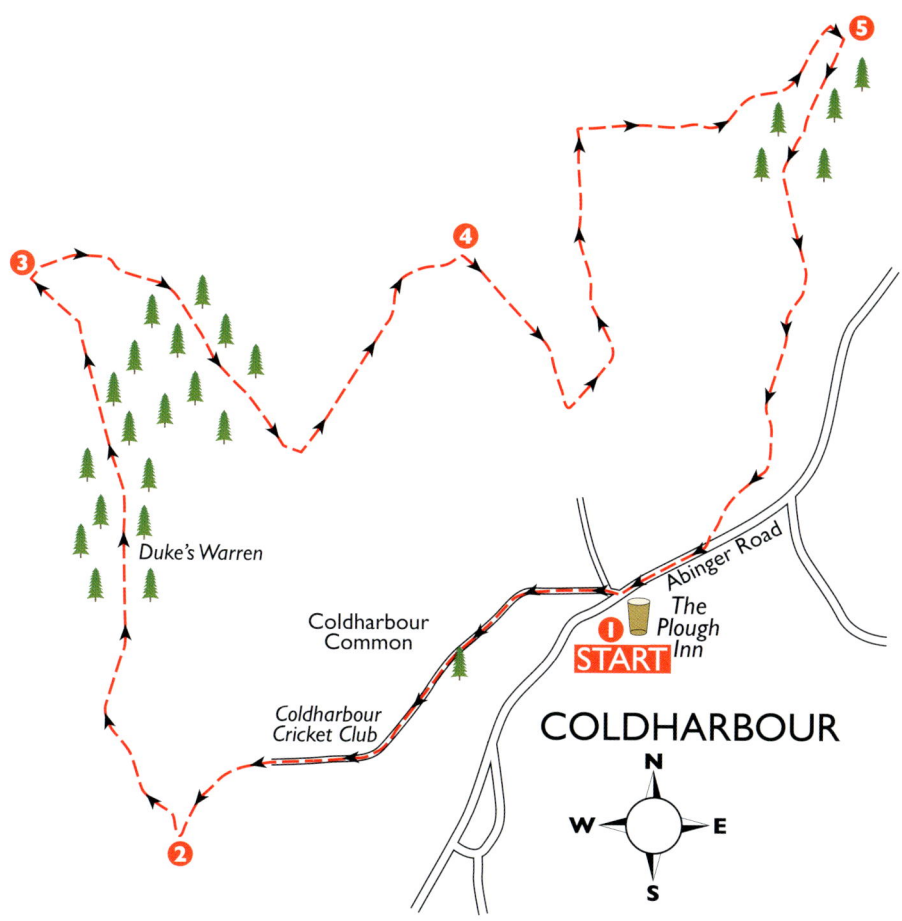

Meander along the path through the trees for around ½ mile, listening out for the entrancing birdsong of crossbills and siskins as you go.

3 When you reach an arresting apple tree on the right, turn right through a gate. Keeping right, wind down through a stretch of the pretty woods of **Duke's Warren** to an opening at the bottom, then turn left up the hill. Follow a sweeping path under the trees, past paths on your left and right, and a gate to a big junction where you turn right.

Coldharbour 16

4 When you reach a giant black hitching post, turn left and follow the path to the left of a field. Take the deeply rutted car track next, then bear right to path junction and turn right. Keep right before heading down and up a muddy path, which could be boggy after persistent rain so take care with your footing. When you reach a choice of three paths at the top, take the middle steep one.

5 When you emerge - thankful for flatter ground – at the top, turn right down a path until you reach a big downhill path through trees. Tread carefully down the vertiginous descent, then follow the path around to a pheasant feeding path. Please be prepared for pheasants of all sizes to emerge from the surrounding trees as they are easily scared. Head past the corn field and up to the main **Abinger Road**. Watch out for traffic, then turn right down the hill back to the pub.

Places of Interest Nearby

Coldharbour is a pretty hamlet at the foot of the better-known **Leith Hill** nearby, which has a quintessential Surrey charm that draws in people from far and wide. John Labouchere of Broome Hall built the **church and parsonage house**, while it has become a stopping point for road cyclists and mountain bikers as well as traditional horse riders.

For something a little different, the **Hannah Peschar Sculpture Garden** is a couple of miles south of here. Open from April to October, this innovative destination exhibits works by a diverse range of artists in immaculately tended gardens.
🌐 www.hannahpescharsculpture.com/

Walk 17
FOREST GREEN

Distance: 3 miles (5 km)

Start: The Parrot, Horsham Road, Forest Green, RH5 5RZ.

How to get there: The Parrot is nestled at the southern edge of the beautiful Surrey Hills. You can reach it best by road from Ockley Road to the east and west, B2126 to the north and Horsham Road to the south. Ockley train station is only seven minutes away by taxi, while there are occasional buses from the likes of Cranleigh, Ockley and Capel.

Parking: Park at the pub but please ask permission from the landlord before leaving your car.

Map: OS Explorer 146: Dorking, Box Hill & Reigate.
Grid Ref: TQ123412.

The Parrot is a splendid anchor point for a lovely walk that takes you up through the underrated Leith Hill Wood where the Rhododendron Wood is stunning from as early as February until June. Even though it is a shorter walk, the uphill first stretch will test your lungs before the gratifying descent back down.

Forest Green 17

THE PUB — **THE PARROT** has a long history that undoubtedly adds to its charm. The eclectic menu has an English and Asian influence, while the brilliant aspect of the pub sees the sun moving around from the back in the morning to the front overlooking the quaint green later on. It is extremely popular with walkers, mountain bikers and cyclists.
⊕ www.brunningandprice.co.uk/parrot/homepage
☎ 01306 775790.

The Walk

❶ Head right out of the pub along **Horsham Road** to where it meets the **B2127/Ockley Road**. Turn right keeping to the path across the grass following the road round as it bends right, where you continue along the verge taking care of any traffic. Look out for the car park at the base of **Etherley Copse** on your left. Just before the car park, there is a stile that leads into **Collins Farm**. Climb over the stile and start walking uphill alongside the fence that borders the Copse. You will need to be careful over the next stile as you need to cross planks on the right too. Keep right alongside the Copse border up the next field until you reach another stile. Climb over and cross a small section of woods, then climb over another stile.

❷ Cross the final field until you reach a stile and planks over water that leads into the woods. Make your way up the side of the woods along a footpath that borders a garden on the left. You will come out onto a road where you turn right until you reach a gate to **Leith Hill Rhododendron Wood**. Walk down a little, then turn left into the Wood itself. Keep to the top path and wind your way through the magical rhododendrons, which spring into colourful life from February through until June. When you reach the path to the car park, turn right and then take the next left following the path for 100m. At the next junction, turn right keeping to the path as it meanders around the bottom section of the Wood.

❸ When the path crosses another, turn left and wind your way back towards the entrance. Turn left down the main track that also doubles as a bridleway. Pass a track to your left and keep ahead

Surrey Pub Walks

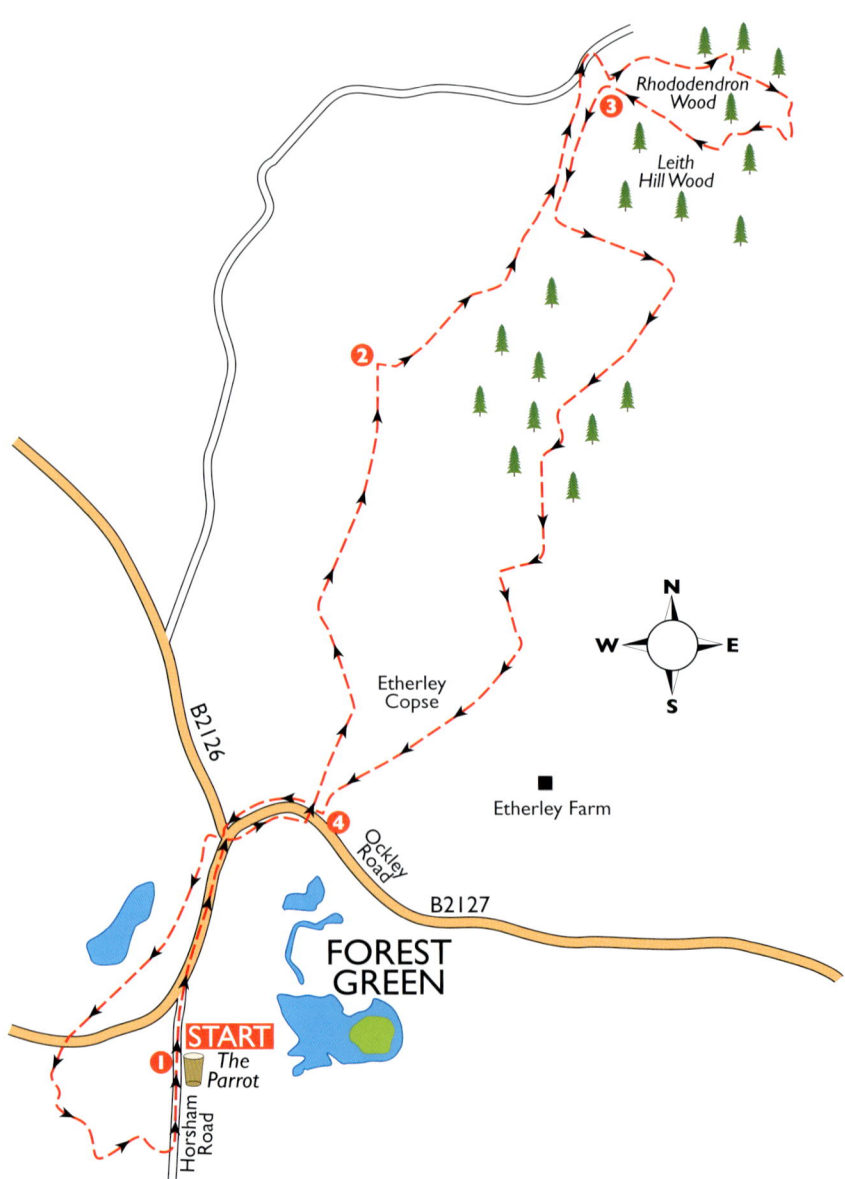

until you reach another track to your left, which you take. When you see the **Etherley Farm Loop** sign, head right. When you reach **Dingwall Wood**, keep left and head down another long

Forest Green

path. Turn right for a bit at the bottom of **Dingwall Wood**, then left down the final track towards the car park where you might be lucky enough to see deer.

4 When you get to the road, turn right carefully around the blind corner. Cross over the road when you get around the bend on to the right-hand verge and carry on down to the stunning **Forest Green Forge** building. Cross **Ockley Road** to the lane that borders the cricket pitch, then bear right of the pavilion over the stream. Cut back left and over another stream bridge before steering right until you can safely take **Horsham Road** back to the **Parrot**.

Places of Interest Nearby

Forest Green is set below the greensand hills that rise up and form at Leith Hill, the highest point in south-eastern England. The **Evelyn Estate** was formed in 1579 and by 1625 included Forest Green with the earliest building dating back to the 15th century. The historic **Forest Green Forge** dates back to the 16th century, operating as a smithy initially and now as a producer of beautiful bespoke metalwork. ⊕ forestgreenforge.co.uk

Walk 18
COULSDON

Distance: 2¼ miles (3.6 km)

Start: The Rambler's Rest, Outwood Lane, Coulsdon, CR5 3NP.

How to get there: The Rambler's Rest pub is nestled in the northeast of Surrey between the towns of Banstead and Coulsdon as well as the village of Kingswood. You can access the car park easily from the west and south in 10 minutes from Junction 8 of the M25 using the A217 and Blackhorse Lane or approach it handily from the north and east via the A217 and A23 with the B2032 between Kingswood and Coulsdon allowing you to reach it from either side. The pub is a 15-minute walk from Chipstead train station, but it is not well served by bus.

Parking: Park at the pub but please ask permission from the landlord before leaving your car.

Map: OS Explorer 146: Dorking, Box Hill & Reigate.
Grid Ref: TQ273575.

This gentle, family-friendly walk is a great entry point to the delights of Surrey. With enough elevation to get the blood pumping and picturesque views across the landscape from

Coulsdon

several points, it's the perfect place for a stroll before or after a stop at the Rambler's Rest.

THE PUB — **THE RAMBLER'S REST** has been both a pub and restaurant over the years. The central garden is a big selling point with punters able to look back up towards Banstead Woods and Chipstead Downs Nature Reserve. The dining area has lots of quiet corners, spacious tables, and intimate spaces along with an inviting fire by the main bar area in the middle.
🌐 www.theramblersrest.co.uk/tablebooking ☎ 01737 552661.

The Walk

❶ Head to the back of the car park of the **Rambler's Rest** where you will find a kissing gate to start your walk. The first part of the walk is the most strenuous as you head uphill until you reach the next kissing gate, where you can take a moment to look back at the wonderful views of the valley that carves its way from Coulsdon through to Kingswood. The next part remains uphill until you reach a path that runs across the ridge line, which is where you turn left and walk past brambles on either side.

❷ The next flat part sees a fence on your left that winds its way uphill northwest onto the **Banstead Woods Nature Trail**. Bear right, then bear left until you reach a pond with a bench on the right which provides a welcome point to take a breather.

❸ Turn right on a long stretch of wooded path past a big pile of logs. The next long stretch takes you past more brambles that will bear fruit in season. Head past two right turns and go downhill for around 100m. Turn right on to a wide bridle path that takes you past benches that have been built in memory of walkers. Once you see a fox sign on the right, you will be near the magical **Narnia wardrobe** carved out of standing deadwood by talented chainsaw sculptor Ella from The Tree Pirates that forms

Surrey Pub Walks

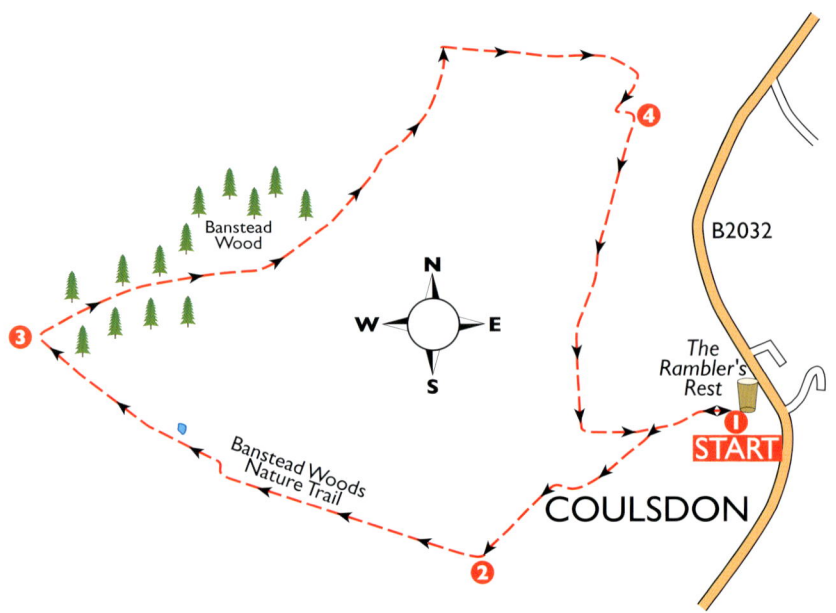

part of the marvellous Narnia trail inspired by C. S. Lewis' classic children's tale *The Lion, the Witch and the Wardrobe*. You can pass through the tempting door of the wardrobe and wooden coats within to the other side where your imagination can do the rest. There are some other wooden delights to be found off the main path, so keep on searching them out. If you carry straight on, then you will soon come across the woodchip conservation area on the left where people have been undertaking coppicing and dead hedging in a bid to replicate old forestry techniques. Bear right back towards the ridge line, then head down a small, steep chute that leads on to a tighter path that runs parallel to the main one.

❹ The ground consists of more flint here so take care in making your way along it as well as on the muddier parts following rain. There are several spots where you can peek through the trees to take in the glorious views across the valley before you head back down towards the pub. Watch your footing as you turn left down the steep slope for the final 200m or so until it flattens out to the kissing gate and the car park beyond. There is a large outside area to enjoy during the sunnier months or head inside to cosy up by the roaring fire by the bar, which leads to the restaurant.

Places of Interest Nearby

Banstead Woods – the main setting for the walk – was a deer park in medieval times, with both King Edward I and II having gifted it to their wives and used it for hunting. Owned by the local council since 1934, the 250 acres of ancient woodland on chalk, clay with flints and dry valley gravel is designated as a Site of Special Scientific Interest (SSSI) by Natural England. Oak, ash and hazel trees dominate, with shrubs such as field maple and goat willow dotted around, as well as carpets of bluebells in spring and fungi in autumn and winter.
⊕ www.woodlandtrust.org.uk/visiting-woods/woods/banstead-woods

Walk 19
BLETCHINGLEY

Distance: 4 miles (6.3 km)

Start: The Bletchingley Arms, 2 High St, Bletchingley, RH1 4PE.

How to get there: The Bletchingley Arms pub is situated in the village of Bletchingley, which is a conservation area with timber-framed buildings from the late Middle Ages in a designated area of outstanding natural beauty (AONB). It is located between the villages of Nutfield to the west and Godstone to the east on the A25, while you can also access it easily from Junction 6 of the M25 through Godstone as well as Outwood Lane from the south. The nearest train stations are Nutfield and Godstone, while there are regular buses nearby too.

Parking: Park at the pub if visiting or on the High Street near the church and Village Stores.

Map: OS Explorer 146: Dorking, Box Hill & Reigate.
Grid Ref: TQ329507.

Bletchingley 19

A **moderately challenging walk,** with spectacular early views down across Castlehill Farm and Sandhills Lodge, and (during summer and autumn) a lovely section through head-high corn near the end. It can get boggy after persistent rain, so either wear a decent pair of boots or save it for the sunnier months.

THE BLETCHINGLEY ARMS is a dog-friendly pub that caters to pretty much everyone – they serve pub favourites along with a dedicated vegetarian, vegan, NGCI (No Gluten-Containing Ingredients) and children's menu. The spacious  pub garden and large play area is well suited to families, while there is also a children's playground over the other side of the road to entertain the little ones. Al fresco dining is possible all year round with covered tables under their tent, heated dining huts and garden pods.
🌐 www.baronspubs.com/bletchingleyarms ☎ 01883 740142.

The Walk

❶ From **The Bletchingley Arms** turn right or, if you've parked on the **High Street**, stand with your back to the church and turn left, then cut down **Outwood Lane** until the houses peter out on the right-hand side of the road and you reach a footpath on the right. Head up the steps and follow the footpath until you get to the end of **Castle Square** road and see a signed footpath to your left.

❷ Keep to the right-hand edge of the field and follow the footpath down as it gets progressively narrower and watch where you place your feet as there is a barbed wire fence on the left. Spare a moment to take in those breathtaking views back down across **Castlehill Farm** and **Sandhills Lodge**, then head downhill through a pretty wooded section with overhanging trees and round to the left until you get alongside a field (often containing cattle). This is the one area that gets very boggy if there has been persistent rain so take care. Step over the stile then bear right up past some farm buildings and through a gate. Enjoy a gentle

Surrey Pub Walks

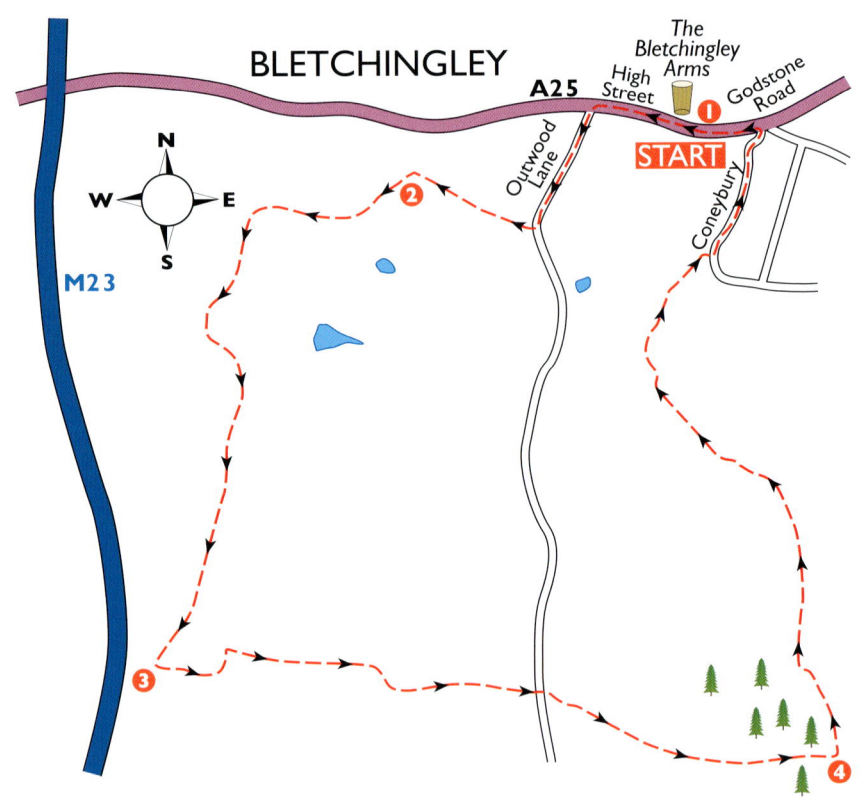

stroll across fields, passing over a stream, until you come close to the M23.

❸ Do not follow the path underneath the motorway but instead turn left across another field and through a gate. Once in the next field turn left and follow the field edge round to the right as it skirts the bottom of **Sandhills Farm**. Pass through another gate then up towards a gate where a water trough lies for horses, which you might be lucky enough to meet. The next bucolic section sees you pass by beehives and an orchard to your left, then bear right with the trees on your left until you reach another gate. Pass through a small gate and head across a field towards another small gate. There are often sheep in the field so if you have a dog with you make sure it is on a lead. Cross the field to

Bletchingley 19

a gate and a road. Cross with care into a driveway opposite. Keep left until you find another footpath that meanders alongside **Nutfield Brook**. When you reach the woods, follow the path slightly deeper until you reach the other side.

4 Before emerging from the trees turn sharp left back up towards **Bletchingley** crossing a small stream bridge with care. Wind your way through the woods until you come out into a field, which was full of head-high corn when we walked the route. Amble across the path cut into the field, then duck down through some trees to reach a further field where you keep right into another field where you reach another stretch of woods to your left. Head through the wood, coming out the other side of **Crookedfield Shaw**, then head across another field to its far left-hand corner. You will reach another wooded area where you turn left up a gully of sorts until you reach a stretch of footpath, which could have blackberry bushes crowding your progress at certain times of year so be careful. Bear left following the path towards the housing estate, passing between the houses. Turn right at the end of the path, then left down **Coneybury** past the primary school. Follow the road round then turn left onto a footpath that climbs back up left alongside **Godstone Road** and back to the pub and **High Street** beyond.

Places of Interest Nearby

Bletchingley was first recorded in the Domesday Book in 1086 and a castle was built here soon after the Norman Conquest as the Surrey base of the de Clare family. The earliest houses to survive substantially intact are 15th-century with **Brewer Street Farmhouse** – a timber-framed and jettied hall house – being a good example of this style of building.

A 15-minute drive down the road you'll find the marvellous **British Wildlife Centre**. It's essentially a zoo dedicated to Britain's own wildlife species, including badgers, otters, free-ranging red squirrels, owls and more.
⊕ www.britishwildlifecentre.co.uk

Walk 20

Limpsfield Chart

Distance: 3 miles (5 km)

Start: The Carpenters Arms, Tally Road, Limpsfield Chart, Oxted, Surrey, RH8 0TG.

How to get there: The Carpenters Arms is located 10 minutes from Junction 6 of the M25 to the west and 15 minutes from Junction 5 of the M25 to the east, while you can easily access it from the B269 that runs off the nearby A25. The nearest train stations running from London Victoria and London Bridge are Oxted seven minutes away to the east by taxi and the same distance to Edenbridge from the south, while you can also catch 236, 410 and 594 buses.

Parking: Park at the Carpenters Arms if visiting, or roadside on Tally Road just outside the pub.

Map: OS Explore 147: Sevenoaks & Tonbridge.
Grid Ref: TQ425518.

Limpsfield Chart 20

This woodland walk on the Surrey/Kent border should take around an hour and guides you through the gorgeous, calming trees of the High Chart in a satisfying loop back to the Carpenters Arms where you can sample top-notch food and real ales from the nearby Westerham Brewery.

THE PUB A quintessential country pub, **THE CARPENTERS ARMS** dates back to the 1800s and used to be a stop on the way to London, with a hitching post for horses outside. It prides itself on using fresh ingredients from local suppliers to provide tasty British meals, with vegan and vegetarian options available. The large beer garden and patio area are popular in the summer months. ⊕ www.carpenterslimpsfield.co.uk ☎ 01883 722209.

The Walk

❶ Head left out of the pub down **Tally Road** and over **Moorhouse Road** into **Limpsfield Common**. Stroll down the footpath, ignoring paths to the left and right, and cross over one large track until you reach the next track. Here you turn left, then right

Surrey Pub Walks

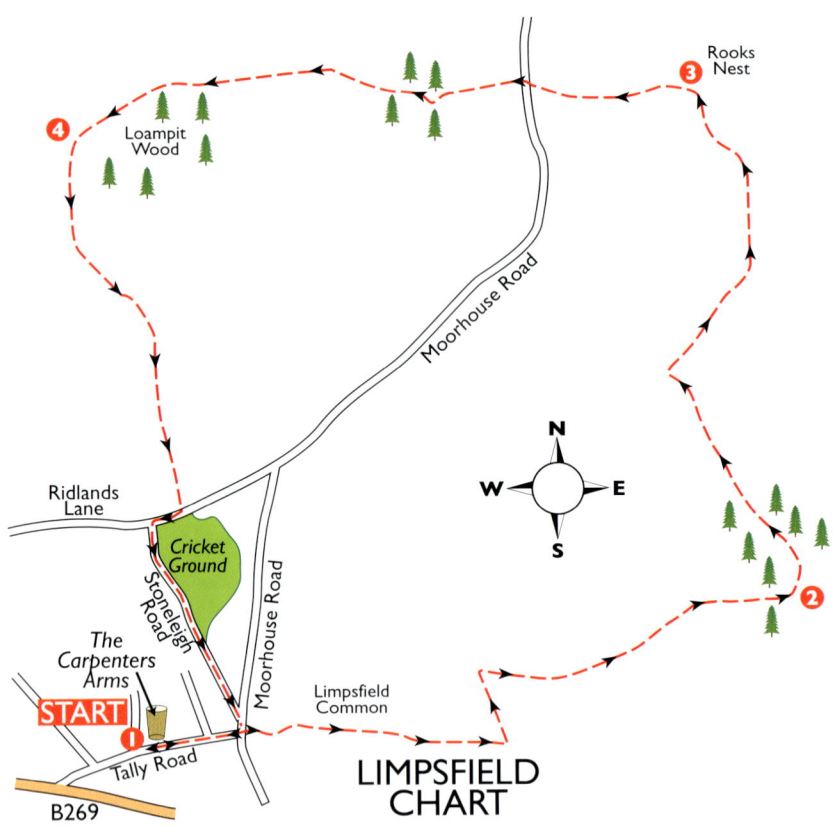

in 100m onto a generous bridleway where you need to keep your ears and eyes out for horses. Cross straight over another track and continue until the end and a junction of paths.

❷ Don't head over to the track ahead, but turn left back into woods staying on the bridleway. Follow that over one track, then turn right at the next junction. Bear right at the next junction with the field edge to your right and follow the track up a hill past **Rooks Nest** on your right where it becomes a bridleway again.

❸ Bend left and amble down to a gate and then cross over **Moorhouse Road** into the car park on the right and the footpath at the back of it. Follow this through a charming open fern

Limpsfield Chart 20

clearing and through a levered gate into a field. Cross the field and head through another levered gate back into the woods. Head right up the hill at the fork and follow the bridleway with **Loampit Wood** to your left.

4 Turn left at the next junction and bear left at the next one past **Cronklands** on your left to get back to **Ridlands Lane**. Keep to the right of the idyllic cricket pitch, and head up **Stoneleigh Road**. Turn right when you reach **Tally Road** to return to the pub.

Places of Interest Nearby

Limpsfield Chart is a few minutes south of **Limpsfield** itself, bordering **Limpsfield Common**, a National Trust area popular with dog walkers and families.

Just over the border in Kent is historic **Chartwell**. The former home of Sir Winston Churchill, it is now cared for by the National Trust and the whole place remains just as it would have been when he lived there.

⊕ www.nationaltrust.org.uk/visit/kent/chartwell

OTHER TITLES FROM COUNTRYSIDE BOOKS

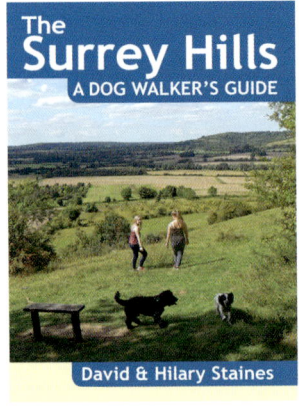

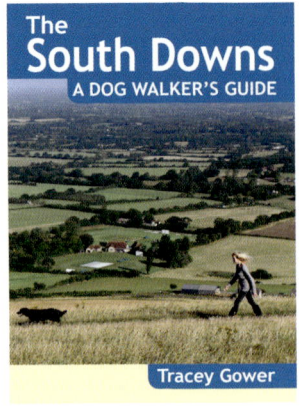

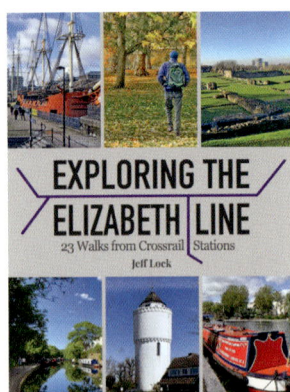

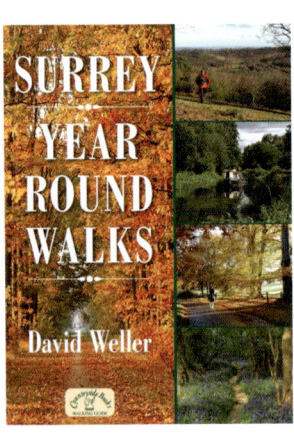
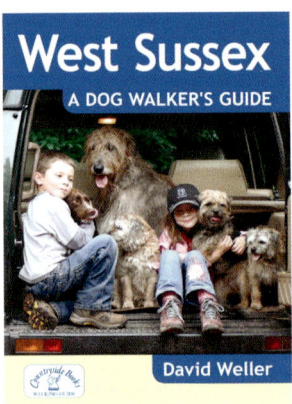

To see the full range of books by Countryside Books please visit
www.countrysidebooks.co.uk

Follow us on   @CountrysideBooks